# SHARKS
# AND OTHER DEADLY
# OCEAN CREATURES

# VISUAL ENCYCLOPEDIA

# CONTENTS

**1**

**2**

## DEVILS OF THE DARK 52

## KILLERS BETWEEN THE TIDES 72

**5**

## MUSCLE-MOUTHED GULPERS 90

### PREDATOR POWER

This scale depends on prey size and the possible danger a predator poses to humans.

Predators that feed on planktonic animals; also parasites that may not kill their victims.

Predators that target small invertebrates and small fish, up to the size of mackerel.

Predators that target and kill medium-sized prey, bigger than mackerel.

Predators that kill small or medium-sized prey, but have venom that could kill bigger animals.

Predators that target large prey up to the size of big mammals, potentially humans.

**6**

## CRUISERS AND CHASERS 104

### SCALES AND SIZES

Profiles of sharks and other creatures have scale drawings to indicate their size.

20.3 cm (8 in)     1.8 m (6 ft)     1.8 m (6 ft)

**7**

**8**

# 1 PRIMEVAL PREDATORS

Sharks first swam the oceans well before the time of the dinosaurs, but other meat-eaters have hunted in these waters even longer. Some prehistoric predators, such as reptilian ichthyosaurs, were quite different from creatures alive today, but others were the ancestors of living animals, including sharks. A few primeval predators, such as the frilled shark, still lurk in the ocean depths.

# SEA
# LAMPREY

*Petromyzon marinus*

## DATA FILE

 **PREDATOR POWER**
 ❗ ● ● ● ●

 **SIZE**: Up to 90 cm (35.4 in) long

 **DISTRIBUTION**: Coastal waters of North Atlantic Ocean and western Mediterranean Sea

 **DIET**: Larvae are filter-feeders; adults feed as parasites on blood of other fish

Lampreys are jawless fish that have scarcely changed in hundreds of millions of years. Like most other lampreys, the adult sea lamprey – the biggest of all – is a blood-sucking parasite of other fish. Adults migrate into rivers to breed, where their eggs hatch into a kind of filter-feeding larva called an ammocoete – found only in lampreys.

Rings of pointed, horn-like teeth scrape at the side of prey to draw blood

Sucker-like, jawless mouth clamps on to side of fish

**Sea lamprey, side view**

The sea lamprey may **sometimes attack whales** or dolphins.

Primeval predators

10

# DEVONIAN
# PLACODERM
*Dunkleosteus* sp.

***Dunkleosteus*, side view**

Hinged connection between head and body

*Dunkleosteus's* **bite strength** may have rivalled that of a great white shark.

Massive, sharp jaws had the strength to bite through prey that had thick armour

The armour-plated placoderms were among the first vertebrates with biting jaws, and so were the first predators to dominate the oceans before the evolution of modern sharks. Their jaws actually worked more like a giant beak. Massive *Dunkleosteus*, known from its fossilized head and body shields, was an early top predator from the Devonian Period (419–358 MYA).

## DATA FILE

 **PREDATOR POWER**

 **SIZE**: Up to 6 m (19.7 ft) long

 **DISTRIBUTION**: Oceans and seas in areas now in North America, Europe, and northern Africa

 **DIET**: Fish and large invertebrates, including those with armour

Primeval predators

# DEVONIAN
## SHARK
*Cladoselache sp.*

This small-toothed shark may have **swallowed prey whole**.

*Cladoselache* belongs to a group of prehistoric sharks that existed in the Devonian Period (419–358 MYA) and which became extinct well before modern sharks evolved. They had some features that set them apart from later sharks, such as sparsely-scaled skin, but they were formidable ocean hunters, and could swim at great speed.

# DEVONIAN
## SHARK
*Stethacanthus sp.*

Anvil-shaped "spine brush"

The remarkable "spine brush" on the back of this early shark from the Devonian Period was made up of a tight bundle of hard, mineralized rods that seemed to spring from the base of the front dorsal fin. The fact that only male sharks had this structure may mean its purpose was to attract mates.

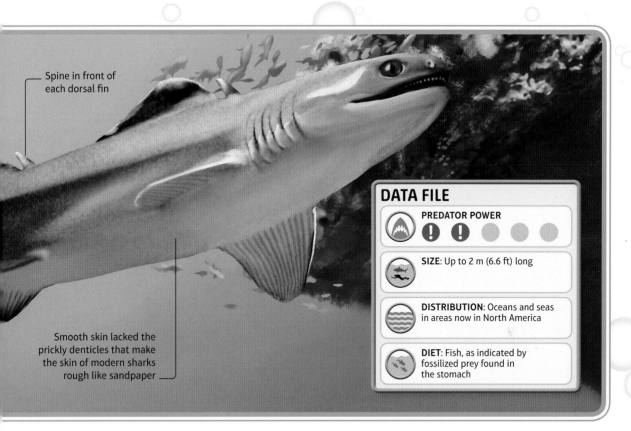

Spine in front of each dorsal fin

Smooth skin lacked the prickly denticles that make the skin of modern sharks rough like sandpaper

## DATA FILE

**PREDATOR POWER**

**SIZE**: Up to 2 m (6.6 ft) long

**DISTRIBUTION**: Oceans and seas in areas now in North America

**DIET**: Fish, as indicated by fossilized prey found in the stomach

Pectoral fins carried a **long whip** of an uncertain function.

## DATA FILE

**PREDATOR POWER**

**SIZE**: Up to 1 m (3.3 ft) long

**DISTRIBUTION**: Oceans and seas in areas now in North America and Europe

**DIET**: Probably fish and crustaceans

# CARBONIFEROUS
## SHARK
*Falcatus falcatus*

Males and females of this shark from the Carboniferous Period (358–298 MYA) looked very different. Only males had the unusual, forward-pointing head spine. It had disproportionately big eyes, perhaps suggesting it was an active predator that relied on good vision to catch or ambush its prey in cloudy water.

# PREHISTORIC EEL-LIKE
## SHARK
*Xenacanthus* sp.

This shark's spine may have been **venomous**.

The long-bodied fossils of this fish show that it might have swum like an eel. This shark from the Permian Period (298–252 MYA) differed from all living sharks in that it had an elongated dorsal fin running along the length of its back, which was connected to the tail fin. Unusually for sharks, it seems to have lived in swampy areas rather than in the ocean.

Primeval predators

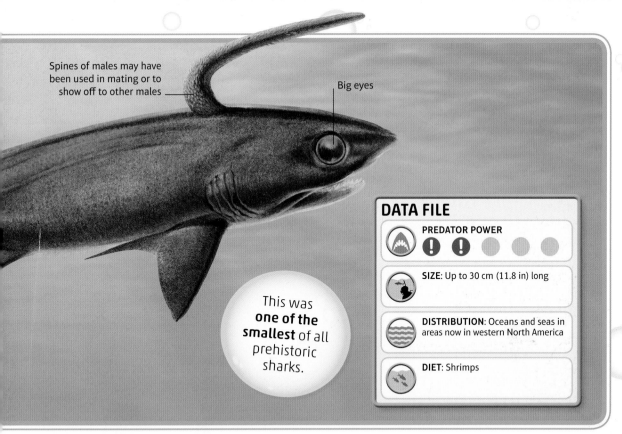

Spines of males may have been used in mating or to show off to other males

Big eyes

This was **one of the smallest** of all prehistoric sharks.

## DATA FILE

**PREDATOR POWER**
! !

**SIZE**: Up to 30 cm (11.8 in) long

**DISTRIBUTION**: Oceans and seas in areas now in western North America

**DIET**: Shrimps

Spine projecting from back of head

Large pectoral fin typical of sharks

## DATA FILE

**PREDATOR POWER**
! !

**SIZE**: Up to 1 m (3.3 ft) long

**DISTRIBUTION**: Swamps, lakes, and rivers in areas now in USA, Europe, and India

**DIET**: Probably fish and small crustaceans

Primeval predators

# HYBODONT
# SHARK
*Hybodus* sp.

Of all the sharks that appeared before the dinosaurs, *Hybodus*, from the Permian to Cretaceous Periods, was one of the most similar to modern sharks and its fossils are widespread. It had sharp front teeth for grabbing prey and blunter ones at the back for crunching, similar to modern snail-eating sharks.

*Hybodus's skeleton was **more bone-like** than in other sharks.*

Sharp spine in front of each dorsal fin, as in some modern sharks

Cutting and grinding teeth in large jaws for grasping and crushing prey

Torpedo-shaped body similar to modern sharks

Primeval predators

## DATA FILE

 **PREDATOR POWER**

 **SIZE**: Up to 2 m (6.6 ft) long

 **DISTRIBUTION**: Shallow seas and freshwaters worldwide

 **DIET**: Probably fish and invertebrates, including hard-shelled prey

16

# SHARPNOSE
# SEVENGILL SHARK

*Heptranchias perlo*

Large eyes

One of just two species of living sharks with seven gills (the other being the broadnose sevengill shark), this hunter is also one of the smallest of the living "primitive" sharks. The sharpnose sevengill spends much of its time in deep water, but is speedy enough to prey on other small sharks, and has enlarged eyes to help it see in dark water.

Seven gill slits unlike most sharks, which have five

The sharpnose sevengill is **known to bite** sometimes when caught.

## DATA FILE

 **PREDATOR POWER**
! ! ! ● ●

 **SIZE:** Up to 1.4 m (4.6 ft) long

 **DISTRIBUTION:** Coastal waters of Atlantic, Indian, and Pacific oceans, and Mediterranean Sea

 **DIET:** Fish (including other small sharks), squid, and cuttlefish

Primeval predators

# BLUNTNOSE SIXGILL SHARK
*Hexanchus griseus*

Single dorsal fin near the rear, like in other primeval sharks

Six gill slits on the side of the body, unlike most sharks, which have five

This is one of the **most globally widespread** of all sharks.

The biggest living primeval shark, the bluntnose sixgill shuns the sunshine and sticks instead to deep, darker waters. It stays close to the bottom and usually only rises upwards at night. Sometimes it follows migrating fish into shallow bays that are dimmed by blooms of plankton, grabbing the occasional seal along the way.

## DATA FILE

**PREDATOR POWER**

**SIZE**: Up to 4.8 m (15.7 ft) long

**DISTRIBUTION**: Deep waters in oceans worldwide and Mediterranean Sea

**DIET**: Fish (including other sharks), squid, crustaceans, and sometimes seals

Primeval predators

# BROADNOSE
# SEVENGILL SHARK
*Notorynchus cepedianus*

Blunt,
pointed snout

Broadnose
sevengills
team up and
**work together**
to hunt seals.

Dark spots are common,
while some sharks may
have white spots on
darker backgrounds

Unlike other living primeval sharks, the broadnose sevengill likes to prowl along coastlines. Here, where the churned-up waters are murky, this hunter relies on poor visibility to take its prey by surprise. It even pokes its head out of the water to watch for prey, such as seals, closer to shore.

## DATA FILE

 **PREDATOR POWER**

 **SIZE**: Up to 3 m (9.8 ft) long

 **DISTRIBUTION**: Temperate coastal waters of the Americas, South Africa, Asia, and Australasia

 **DIET**: Fish (including other sharks), seals, and dolphins

Primeval predators

# FRILLED SHARK

*Chlamydoselachus anguineus*

The frilled shark resembles a storybook serpent. It swims slowly by rippling its long body, but stays in deep, dark water, so is rarely seen alive. Its mouth is filled with three-pronged teeth that may act like little grappling hooks for grabbing slippery prey, such as squid.

This shark has green eyes, like many others found in deep water

First gill slits meet under the head to form a frill

# SPIRAL-TOOTHED CHIMEROID

*Helicoprion sp.*

Scientists **X-rayed fossils** to work out this hunter's anatomy.

This prehistoric relative of living chimaeras had a spiral blade in the floor of its mouth. The "tooth-whorl" on this blade probably spun backwards as the lower jaw closed, but fossils show no wear on teeth. This suggests that *Helicoprion* fed on soft-bodied prey, such as squid.

Primeval predators

Female frilled sharks may be **pregnant** for as long as **three-and-a-half years**.

Single dorsal fin

Eel-like body

**DATA FILE**

PREDATOR POWER

! ! ! ● ●

**SIZE**: Up to 2 m (6.5 ft) long

**DISTRIBUTION**: Deep-ocean waters worldwide

**DIET**: Fish, including other sharks, and squid

Upper jaw fixed to braincase, like in modern chimaeras

Whorl probably retained its teeth, instead of shedding and replacing them like in modern sharks

**DATA FILE**

PREDATOR POWER

! ! ● ● ●

**SIZE**: Probably up to 4 m (13.1 ft) long

**DISTRIBUTION**: Oceans and seas in areas now in North America, Eurasia, and Australia

**DIET**: Probably soft-bodied prey, such as squid

Primeval predators

# CARBONIFEROUS
# SPINY "SHARK"
*Acanthodes* sp.

Spiny "sharks", from the Carboniferous Period (358–298 MYA), had strong spines to support their fins. However, these were not true sharks. Their spines were made of bone, suggesting that the animals might have been related to bony fish, rather than to cartilaginous sharks. They also lacked teeth, so they probably filtered plankton rather than biting prey.

Body covered in tiny scales

# CRETACEOUS
# CHIMAERA
*Ischyodus bifurcatus*

Like living chimaeras, males had a long projection (tentaculum) for grasping females during mating

Even though this fish swam in the oceans in the Cretaceous Period (145–66 MYA), it was remarkably similar to the modern ratfish, a related chimaera that is common in oceans today. This suggests that, as a group, chimaeras have changed very little in more than 70 million years of evolution.

The **spiny fins** of this fish may have **deterred bigger predators**.

Each fin was supported by a single bony spine

## DATA FILE

**PREDATOR POWER**
!

**SIZE:** Up to 30 cm (11.8 in) long

**DISTRIBUTION:** Oceans and seas worldwide

**DIET:** Probably small marine invertebrates and other planktonic animals

Long, tapering, rat-like tail

Some species of *Ischyodus* **lived** almost **to the present day**.

## DATA FILE

**PREDATOR POWER**
! !

**SIZE:** Up to 1 m (3.3 ft) long

**DISTRIBUTION:** Oceans and seas in areas now in North America

**DIET:** Probably hard-shelled invertebrates, such as molluscs and crustaceans

Primeval predators

# AUSTRALIAN PLOUGHNOSE
# CHIMAERA
*Callorhinchus milii*

Shimmering skin

Big pectoral fins
flap like wings and
propel the fish

Hoe-shaped snout is
packed with sensors for
detecting buried prey

Chimaeras' toothplates are not shed like shark teeth, but **keep growing**.

Most chimaeras are deep-water fish, but this one prefers to swim in the shallower waters along coastlines. The Australian ploughnose chimaera uses its peculiar, hoe-shaped snout to probe the mud and sense the activity of buried, hard-shelled, invertebrate prey. It is sometimes called a ghost shark because of its shimmery skin.

## DATA FILE

 **PREDATOR POWER**

 **SIZE**: Up to 1.3 m (4.3 ft) long

 **DISTRIBUTION**: Coastal ocean waters around southern Australia and New Zealand

 **DIET**: Mainly molluscs, such as clams, and other bottom-living invertebrates

Primeval predators

24

# PACIFIC LONGNOSE
# CHIMAERA
*Rhinochimaera pacifica*

Spear-shaped snout
is half the length
of the body

This bizarre-looking hunter is little known and is usually seen only as a curiosity when fishing nets are brought to the surface. The precise purpose of this chimaera's long, spear-shaped snout is not well understood, but, like other chimaeras, its sensors probably help this bottom-living fish find buried invertebrate prey.

Broad, wing-like,
pectoral fins

Gill openings are covered by
a flap called an operculum,
as in all chimaeras

This chimaera
lives in
**deep-ocean
troughs**.

## DATA FILE

 **PREDATOR POWER**

 **SIZE**: Up to 1.6 m (5.2 ft) long

 **DISTRIBUTION**: Deep-ocean waters around Japan, East Asia, Australasia, and Peru

 **DIET**: Probably hard-shelled invertebrates, such as crabs and molluscs

# RABBITFISH
*Chimaera monstrosa*

The rabbitfish belongs to a group of fish called chimaeras. Like in sharks, their skeleton is made from cartilage. However, they split away from sharks and rays over 100 million years before dinosaurs appeared. They differ in having a protective shield, called an operculum, covering their gill opening, and grinding tooth-plates, instead of cutting blades, to crush their prey.

Long, mildly-venomous dorsal fin spine inflicts painful wound

Large eyes to see in deep, dark waters

Snout packed with sensors to help detect bottom-living prey

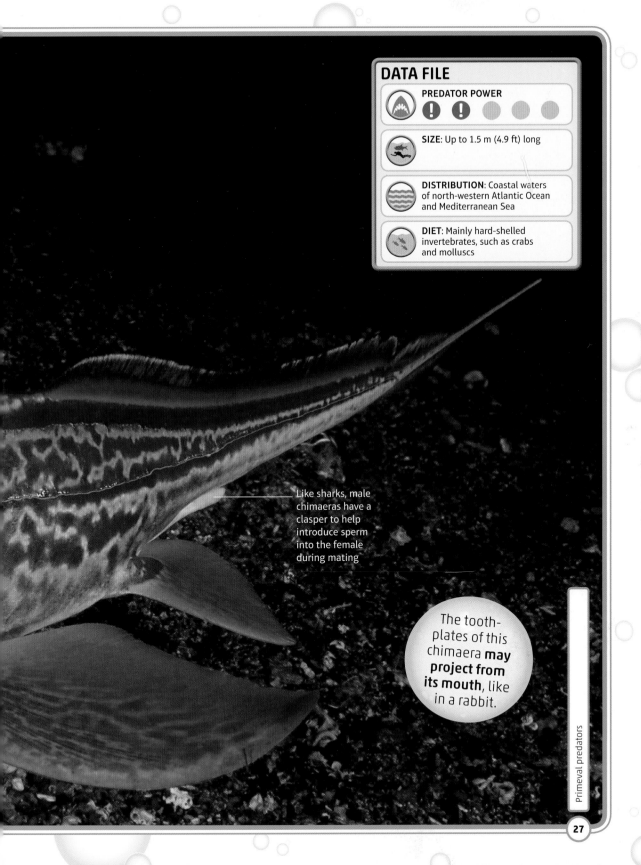

PREDATOR POWER

SIZE: Up to 1.5 m (4.9 ft) long

DISTRIBUTION: Coastal waters of north-western Atlantic Ocean and Mediterranean Sea

DIET: Mainly hard-shelled invertebrates, such as crabs and molluscs

Like sharks, male chimaeras have a clasper to help introduce sperm into the female during mating

The tooth-plates of this chimaera **may project from its mouth**, like in a rabbit.

# GIANT JURASSIC
# BONY FISH
*Leedsichthys problematicus*

The mega-sized *Leedsichthys* was a bony fish, rather than a cartilaginous shark, but its lifestyle was probably similar to the unrelated, modern-day whale shark. Its huge mouth contained gill-rakers for straining small animals from the ocean water. So, like the whale shark, this giant from the Jurassic Period (201–145 MYA) was a gentle filter-feeder.

Enormous set of spiny gill-rakers in mouth filtered plankton

# ALLIGATOR
# GAR
*Atractosteus spatula*

Dorsal fin set far back on long body

Hardened, diamond-shaped scales, like those found only in certain primitive groups of bony fish

One of the biggest fish of North America's swamps, the alligator gar is a formidable ambush predator. While it grabs prey using the double lining of sharp teeth in its jaws, the hardened scales on its body act like armour to protect it from attacks from other animals. It can even breathe in air to supplement the oxygen it gets from the water.

Primeval predators

## DATA FILE

**PREDATOR POWER**
❗

**SIZE:** Up to 17 m (55.8 ft) long

**DISTRIBUTION:** Oceans and seas in areas now in Europe and South America

**DIET:** Probably planktonic animals, such as small fish and invertebrates

Long, scythe-shaped pectoral fins

*Leedsichthys* was the **largest bony fish** that has ever existed.

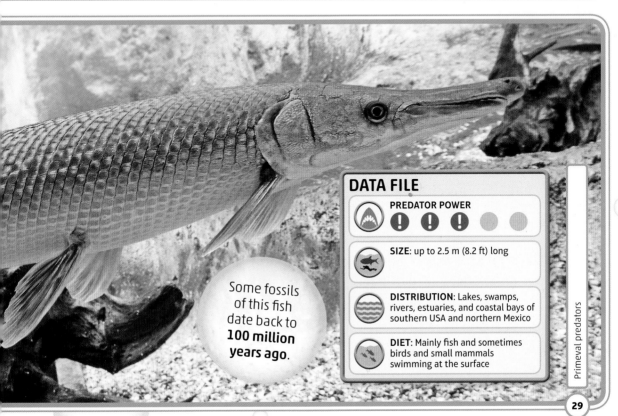

Some fossils of this fish date back to **100 million years ago**.

## DATA FILE

**PREDATOR POWER**
❗ ❗ ❗

**SIZE:** up to 2.5 m (8.2 ft) long

**DISTRIBUTION:** Lakes, swamps, rivers, estuaries, and coastal bays of southern USA and northern Mexico

**DIET:** Mainly fish and sometimes birds and small mammals swimming at the surface

# COELACANTH
*Latimeria chalumnae*

When the first coelacanth was discovered among a fisherman's catch in 1938, it caused a sensation. Before this find, scientists thought this kind of fish had become extinct with the dinosaurs. Together with the lung fish, the coelacanth is one of just a few fish alive today to have the kind of fleshy "lobe-fins" that helped the first vertebrates to conquer land.

Coelacanths have **not changed much** in 390 million years.

Body covered in "armour" of unusually tough scales

Peculiar, three-lobed tail fin found in very few other kinds of fish

Fleshy, lobe-like pelvic fins

## DATA FILE

 **PREDATOR POWER**
 ! !

 **SIZE:** Up to 2 m (6.6 ft) long

 **DISTRIBUTION:** Deep waters and rocky caves of western Indian Ocean

 **DIET:** Fish

# CRETACEOUS
# PLESIOSAUR
*Albertonectes vanderveldei*

The prehistoric oceans were home to two main groups of marine reptiles – the ichthyosaurs and the plesiosaurs. Unlike the ichthyosaurs, the plesiosaurs swallowed stones to counteract the buoyancy of their lungs. They might have done this so they could rest on the ocean floor to grab passing prey. Many plesiosaurs had a long neck to help them swipe at shoals of fish – and *Albertonectes* had the longest neck of them all.

*Albertonectes* had **76 vertebrae** in its neck.

Neck was 7 m (23 ft) long

Two pairs of flippers propelled the animal

Small, pointed teeth probably grabbed soft-bodied prey

## DATA FILE

**PREDATOR POWER**
 ! ! !

**SIZE:** Up to 18 m (59.1 ft) long

**DISTRIBUTION:** Oceans and seas in areas now in North America

**DIET:** Probably fish and soft-bodied, swimming invertebrates

Primeval predators

# JURASSIC
# ICHTHYOSAUR
*Stenopterygius* sp.

The ichthyosaurs of the Jurassic Period (201–145 MYA) were among the first big groups of predatory marine vertebrates to breathe air. *Stenopterygius* and other ichthyosaurs would keep coming to the water surface to breathe. These reptiles evolved as dolphin-shaped fish-eaters with a fish-like tail. Unlike most other reptiles, they gave birth to live young in the water.

*Stenopterygius* could probably swim as **fast as a modern-day tuna**.

Single dorsal fin

Long, pointed snout, filled with sharp teeth for grabbing slippery prey

Two pairs of flippers for swimming

## DATA FILE

 **PREDATOR POWER**
! ! ! ● ●

 **SIZE:** Up to 4 m (13.1 ft) long

 **DISTRIBUTION:** Oceans and seas in areas now in Europe

 **DIET:** Fish and belemnoids (prehistoric relatives of modern squid)

Primeval predators

32

# MEGALODON
*Carcharodon megalodon*

Teeth could have been up to five times bigger than those of the great white

Torpedo-shaped body for speedy swimming

Megalodon may have had the **biggest bite force** of any animal.

The largest shark that ever lived appeared in the Miocene epoch (23–5 MYA), a time when mammals had long since replaced dinosaurs. *Megalodon* was a relatively modern cousin of the great white shark, rather than a genuinely primeval predator. It probably evolved to hunt the whales that had begun to appear in the oceans at that time.

## DATA FILE

**PREDATOR POWER**
! ! ! ! !

**SIZE:** Possibly more than 20 m (65.6 ft) long

**DISTRIBUTION:** Oceans and seas worldwide

**DIET:** Large fish and marine mammals such as whales

# 2

# MUD-ROOTING MONSTERS

Most sharks hunt in the ocean's mid-waters, but some, including angelsharks, have a different lifestyle. They have flat bodies that hug the seabed, skin colours that match their background, and rely on camouflage to catch their prey. Virtually all rays, the closest living relatives of sharks, have made their living this way. Some bony fishes, such as flatfish, are bottom-dwellers too.

# LONGNOSE
# SAWSHARK

*Pristiophorus cirratus*

Sawsharks use their sword-like snout for both sensing and killing prey. The snout is packed with sensors that detect the muscular activity of small animals buried in sand and gravel. Once the prey is roused from its hiding place, the sawshark sweeps its snout from side to side, cutting the unfortunate victim to pieces.

Long, sword-like snout has 19–21 large teeth running along each side

## DATA FILE

 **PREDATOR POWER**

 **SIZE**: Up to 1.5 m (4.9 ft) long

 **DISTRIBUTION**: Shallow coastal waters of western and southern Australia

 **DIET**: Small fish and crustaceans

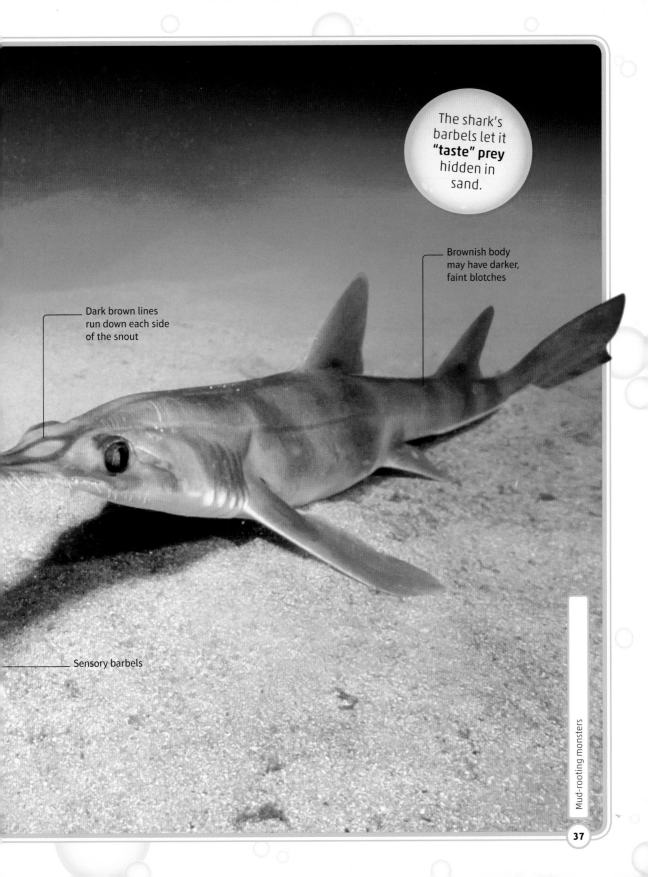

The shark's barbels let it **"taste" prey** hidden in sand.

Brownish body may have darker, faint blotches

Dark brown lines run down each side of the snout

Sensory barbels

# SAND DEVIL

*Squatina dumeril*

Angelsharks are named for their broad pectoral fins, which look like angel's wings. Their behaviour, however, is anything but angelic. When disturbed, the sand devil bites aggressively with its needle-like teeth. In northern parts of its range, it moves inshore close to the coast, but further south it sticks to deeper water.

Plain, grey body may have some darker spots

One of two small dorsal fins near the tail fin

The sand devil gets its name from its **aggressive temperament**.

## DATA FILE

 **PREDATOR POWER**

 **SIZE**: Up to 1.5 m (4.9 ft) long

 **DISTRIBUTION**: Coastal waters of western North America and Caribbean Sea

 **DIET**: Bottom-living fish, crustaceans, and bivalve molluscs, such as clams and mussels

# COMMON
# ANGELSHARK
*Squatina squatina*

Angelsharks look and behave like rays. When prey passes nearby, however, they turn into formidable hunters. They make a grab with lightning-fast jaws, and can even arch their "neck" upwards to help with the catch. This species is found only in Europe, but other angelsharks are found around the world.

White, criss-crossing lines disappear as the shark grows bigger

This shark can strike its prey in **one-tenth of a second**.

Greyish or brownish body peppered with spots

## DATA FILE

 **PREDATOR POWER**

 **SIZE**: Up to 1.8 m (5.9 ft) long

 **DISTRIBUTION**: Shallow coastal waters of Europe and Mediterranean Sea

 **DIET**: Bottom-living fish (especially flatfish and skates), crustaceans, and molluscs

Mud-rooting monsters

# BIG
## SKATE
*Raja binoculata*

Two tiny dorsal fins set far back on tapering tail

One of two eye-like spots on the upper surface of the skate's body gives it the scientific name *binoculata*

Skates make up nearly half of the hundreds of species of rays. The big skate is the biggest one in the waters around North America. Its rigid, pointed snout and triangular "wings" give it the shape of a diamond that is as wide as it is long. It glides gracefully when swimming, but spends more time partly buried in the mud, with just its eyes poking out.

## DATA FILE

 **PREDATOR POWER**

 **SIZE**: Up to 2.4 m (7.9 ft) long

 **DISTRIBUTION**: Coastal waters of western North America

 **DIET**: Fish and crustaceans

# COMMON GUITARFISH

*Rhinobatos rhinobatos*

Guitarfish have high dorsal fins, like sharks, but a flattened, ray-like body. They are more closely related to rays and share their habit of hunting buried animals. The common guitarfish pins down shrimps and other prey on the seabed with its pointed snout, before sucking them into its mouth and crushing them with its molar-like teeth.

## DATA FILE

 **PREDATOR POWER**

 **SIZE**: Up to 1.5 m (4.9 ft) long

 **DISTRIBUTION**: Coastal waters over mud or sand of Mediterranean Sea and eastern Atlantic Ocean

 **DIET**: Bottom-living invertebrates and fish

A **milk-like liquid** inside the mother's womb nourishes unborn pups.

One of two dorsal fins near the rear of the body

Pectoral fins form "wings" on guitar-shaped body

# GIANT
# GUITARFISH
*Rhynchobatus djiddensis*

The dorsal fins of this guitarfish are bigger and more shark-like than those of the related wedgefish, and its pointed snout is longer. When hunting in muddy shallows, the giant guitarfish often comes right up into the surf, making it an easy catch for fishermen. Because it breeds slowly and has a small litter size, over-fished populations take time to recover.

## DATA FILE

 **PREDATOR POWER**

**SIZE**: Up to 3.1 m (10.2 ft) long

**DISTRIBUTION**: Coral reefs and estuaries of Red Sea and Indian Ocean

**DIET**: Crabs, lobsters, bivalves, squid, and small fish

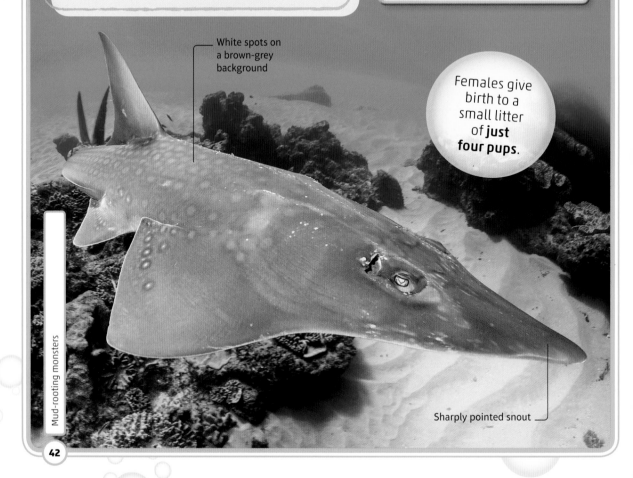

White spots on a brown-grey background

Females give birth to a small litter of **just four pups**.

Sharply pointed snout

# SMALL-TOOTHED SAWFISH
*Pristis pectinata*

This sawfish often swims into the **mouths of rivers**.

Long snout edged with row of teeth running along each side

Eyes much smaller than those of sawsharks

Although this sawfish is similar to sawsharks, its downward-facing gill slits show that it is more closely related to rays. Like the sawsharks, the small-toothed sawfish uses its "saw" as a sense organ as well as a weapon. It sweeps its saw to impale small fish and then scrapes off the injured prey on the sea bottom to eat it.

## DATA FILE

 **PREDATOR POWER**
❗ ❗ ⚫ ⚫ ⚫

 **SIZE:** Up to 7.6 m (24.9 ft) long

 **DISTRIBUTION:** Coastal waters and estuaries of Atlantic, Indian, and Pacific oceans

 **DIET:** Fish and shellfish

Mud-rooting monsters

# MARBLED
# TORPEDO RAY
*Torpedo marmorata*

The torpedo ray stuns prey by firing electric shocks into the water, but it also uses the shocks for self-defence. It arches its belly outwards to make the shock spread out more effectively. It generates up to 200 volts, enough to knock another fish senseless or give a painful jolt to a human.

## DATA FILE

 **PREDATOR POWER**

 **SIZE**: Up to 1 m (3.3 ft) long

 **DISTRIBUTION**: Coastal waters over reefs and seagrass of eastern Atlantic Ocean and Mediterranean Sea

 **DIET**: Bottom-living fish and invertebrates

Round dorsal fins over tail

Marbled pattern camouflages this ray from prey on sea bottom

The electric shock organs of this ray develop **even before they are born**.

# LESSER ELECTRIC RAY
*Narcine bancroftii*

## DATA FILE

 **PREDATOR POWER**

**SIZE:** Up to 60 cm (23.6 in) long

**DISTRIBUTION:** Tropical coastal waters of western Atlantic Ocean and Caribbean Sea

**DIET:** Mainly marine worms

This species belongs to a family of electric rays that are sometimes called numbfish. Numbfish are generally smaller than the related torpedo rays and give weaker electric shocks, more in self-defence, rather than to stun prey. As in torpedo rays, the jaws of the lesser electric ray protrude from its head to grab prey buried in mud and silt.

Rays may use electric shocks to **communicate with one another**.

Snout more pointed than that of torpedo rays

Mud-rooting monsters

# BLUE-SPOTTED
# RIBBONTAIL RAY
*Taeniura lymma*

The strikingly coloured blue-spotted ribbontail ray often rests among rocks or stays buried in sand with just its eyes and sting-bearing tail showing. The sting has one or two backward-pointing, venomous spines that can inflict a painful injury when used in self-defence. Like other rays, this fish smothers bottom-living prey with its flat, disc-like body before eating them.

Small, prickly denticles run down the back

Bright blue spots may help disguise the ray in sun-dappled, shallow water

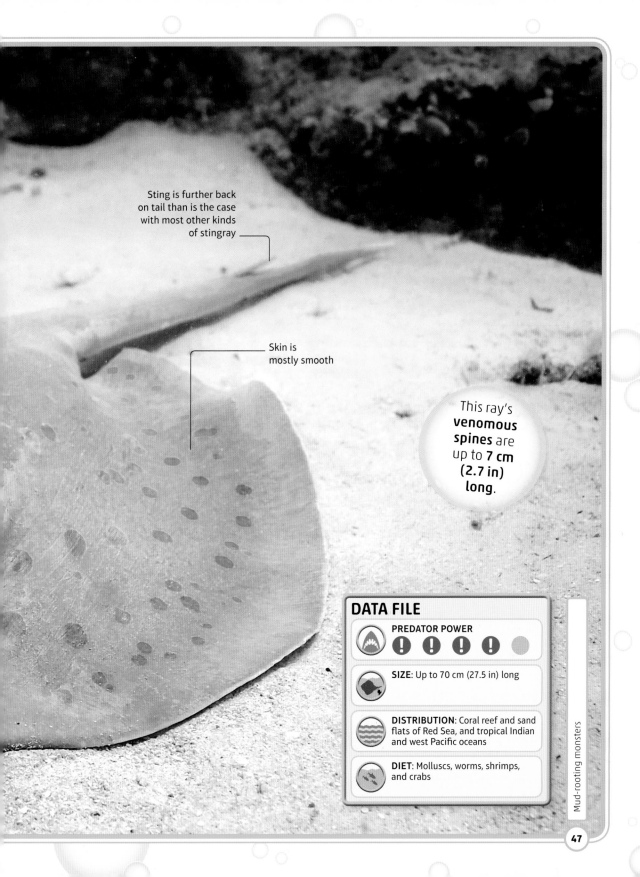

Sting is further back
on tail than is the case
with most other kinds
of stingray

Skin is
mostly smooth

This ray's **venomous spines** are up to **7 cm (2.7 in) long**.

## DATA FILE

**PREDATOR POWER**

**SIZE**: Up to 70 cm (27.5 in) long

**DISTRIBUTION**: Coral reef and sand flats of Red Sea, and tropical Indian and west Pacific oceans

**DIET**: Molluscs, worms, shrimps, and crabs

Mud-rooting monsters

# PEACOCK FLOUNDER

*Bothus mancus*

Both eyes on left side in this left-eyed flatfish

The peacock flounder is a flatfish that can change colour to match its surroundings. Like other flatfish, the young that hatch from eggs look unremarkable. As they grow, they go through a process of physical change whereby their eyes end up on one side of the body. The fish settles down on the seabed with its eyeless side flat on the bottom.

# LESSER WEEVER

*Echiichthys vipera*

Dorsal fin spines are connected to venom glands

Eyes on top of head peer upwards to look out for passing prey

The lesser weever is a particular hazard for anyone walking barefoot on a sandy beach. This little fish buries itself in the sand with just its eyes and dorsal fin poking up. It has sharp, stinging spines, and although the fish is scarcely the size of a goldfish, a sting from those spines can cause terrible pain.

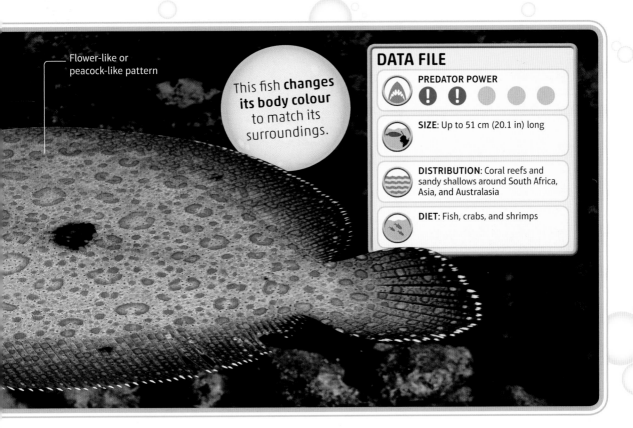

Flower-like or peacock-like pattern

This fish **changes its body colour** to match its surroundings.

## DATA FILE

**PREDATOR POWER**
❗ ❗ ○ ○ ○

**SIZE:** Up to 51 cm (20.1 in) long

**DISTRIBUTION:** Coral reefs and sandy shallows around South Africa, Asia, and Australasia

**DIET:** Fish, crabs, and shrimps

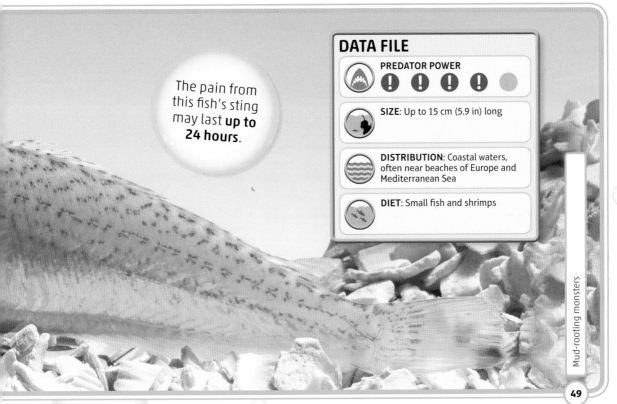

The pain from this fish's sting may last **up to 24 hours**.

## DATA FILE

**PREDATOR POWER**
❗ ❗ ❗ ❗ ○

**SIZE:** Up to 15 cm (5.9 in) long

**DISTRIBUTION:** Coastal waters, often near beaches of Europe and Mediterranean Sea

**DIET:** Small fish and shrimps

Mud-rooting monsters

# SAND STARGAZER

*Dactyloscopus tridigitatus*

**PREDATOR POWER**
 ❗ ❗ ● ● ●

**SIZE**: Up to 9 cm (3.5 in) long

**DISTRIBUTION**: Coastal sand of western Atlantic Ocean and Caribbean Sea

**DIET**: Small fish and invertebrates

The sand stargazer is one of the tiniest fish predators, but it has one of the best tricks for a perfect ambush. The fish gets its name because its eyes point upwards on top of its head. This means it can keep practically its entire body buried in sand, while still keeping watch for any prey passing overhead.

Low dorsal fin on the back runs along the length of the body

Upward-pointing eyes

The male **guards eggs** in its **"armpits"**, under each pectoral fin.

Wide, upward-turned mouth

Mud-rooting monsters

50

# BITING REEF WORM

*Eunice aphroditois*

The biting reef worm grows up to 3 m (9.8 ft) and has jaws that can draw blood from a human finger. This giant waits in the sand, open-mouthed, with its head poking up into the water. When a fish swims within reach, the worm snaps its jaws shut, pulling the prey into its burrow.

Five antennae sense the presence of prey

Sharp-edged jaws can easily slice through fish

This worm's **open jaws can span** a distance of **5 cm (1.9 in)**.

## DATA FILE

 **PREDATOR POWER**

 **SIZE**: Up to 3 m (9.8 ft) long

 **DISTRIBUTION**: Coastal mud and sand of Indian and western Pacific oceans

 **DIET**: Fish, shrimps, other worms, seaweed, and dead matter

Mud-rooting monsters

# 3

# DEVILS OF THE DARK

The most well-known sharks, including the great white, chase their prey near the surface of the ocean. However, more mysterious kinds of predator hunt further down in darker depths. Some remarkable oddities live in this dark world. There are miniature sharks that give off glowing light, and even sneaky parasites that steal lumps of flesh from their unfortunate victims.

# VELVET-BELLY

*Etmopterus spinax*

Brownish upper surface contrasts sharply with darker under surface

The velvet-belly belongs to a group of small, deep-water hunters called lantern sharks. Light-producing organs, called "photophores", pepper the body surface of these sharks, glowing like little lanterns in the dark. They may help to dazzle prey or confuse bigger predators.

The velvet-belly produces **up to 21 pups** in a litter.

# ANGULAR ROUGH SHARK

*Oxynotus centrina*

No other sharks look like rough sharks. This species, like other rough sharks, has high, sail-like dorsal fins – the first just behind the head. An especially oily liver helps to keep this small shark buoyant as it cruises slowly just above the ocean floor, close to its source of favourite food – bottom-living worms.

Devils of the dark

Rounded pelvic fin

Short gills on narrow, spindle-shaped body

Blackish underbelly is covered with light-producing photophores

## DATA FILE

**PREDATOR POWER**

**SIZE:** Up to 41 cm (16.1 in) long

**DISTRIBUTION:** Deep-ocean waters of eastern Atlantic Ocean and western Mediterranean Sea

**DIET:** Small fish, squid, and crustaceans

This shark has especially **rough, prickly skin**.

## DATA FILE

**PREDATOR POWER**

**SIZE:** Up to 1.5 m (4.9 ft) long

**DISTRIBUTION:** Deep coastal waters of eastern Atlantic Ocean and Mediterranean Sea

**DIET:** Mainly worms

Leaf-shaped pectoral fin

Devils of the dark

**55**

# GREENLAND
# SHARK
*Somniosus microcephalus*

The world's coldest oceans bring life into the slow lane. Beneath the Arctic ice, the Greenland shark is the slowest fish for its size and has a lazy taste for carrion (dead animals). Despite its sluggishness, this shark can be a crafty mover when it wants to be. It has even been known to grab reindeer that slip off the ice.

Small eye

## DATA FILE

 **PREDATOR POWER**
    !  !  !  !  !

 **SIZE**: Up to 7.3 m (23.9 ft) long

 **DISTRIBUTION**: Cold, deep coastal waters of North Atlantic and Arctic oceans

 **DIET**: Fish, invertebrates, seabirds, seals, and carrion

This sluggish shark moves and breathes slowly, so has small gill slits

One of two small, similarly sized dorsal fins

Greenland sharks may live for **more than 150 years**.

# PYGMY SHARK

*Euprotomicrus bispinatus*

## DATA FILE

 **PREDATOR POWER**
❗ ❗ ○ ○ ○

 **SIZE**: Up to 27 cm (10.6 in) long

 **DISTRIBUTION**: Patches of deep-ocean water mainly in the southern regions of oceans worldwide

**DIET**: Small squid, fish, and some crustaceans

This tiny hunter is the second-smallest species of shark after the dwarf lantern shark. Each night this fish follows its prey and moves up to the surface, covering a distance of more than 1.6 km (1 mile), before returning to the bottom by morning. This feat is equivalent to a human walking 11 km (6.8 miles) and back every day.

Pale marks on pectoral fins

Narrow body tapers back towards tail

The pygmy shark's underbelly **glows in the dark**.

# COOKIECUTTER SHARK
*Isistius brasiliensis*

Dark collar on throat lacks light-producing organs

Cookiecutter **bite marks** have been found on submarines.

Light-producing organs cover the underside of the body

Although small, the cookiecutter is a terrifying carnivore. Bigger predators may approach the cookiecutter, thinking it is easy prey. However, just as they try to bite, the cookiecutter strikes first. It clamps its razor-sharp teeth into its victim and twists round to remove a mouthful of meat.

## DATA FILE

 **PREDATOR POWER**

 **SIZE**: Up to 50 cm (19.7 in) long

**DISTRIBUTION**: Deep-ocean waters worldwide

 **DIET**: Grabs plugs of flesh from big fish and sometimes from dolphins, whales, and seals

Devils of the dark

# KITEFIN SHARK

*Dalatias licha*

Like many deep-sea sharks, this hunter makes up for its moderate size with bold hunting tactics. The kitefin shark has heavy jaws and huge, serrated teeth, and uses them to lunge at bigger fish, tearing off chunks of flesh. Its oily liver keeps it buoyant, helping it to hover in mid-water as it waits to ambush prey that ventures too close.

Large green eyes, like those in many other sharks found in deep, dark water

Thick lips and powerful jaws

# SPINY DOGFISH

*Squalus acanthias*

The spiny dogfish might be called the piranha of the ocean. It moves in big shoals, and can use its jaws to cut bigger fish to pieces. It grows slowly and may live for more than 100 years – prowling the darkness of deep waters and sometimes coming further inshore.

Short spine at the front edge of each dorsal fin

One of two widely separated, equal-sized dorsal fins

This hunter may **attack** other, **bigger, sharks**.

## DATA FILE

**PREDATOR POWER** ! ! ! ! !

**SIZE:** Up to 1.8 m (5.9 ft) long

**DISTRIBUTION:** Deep waters of most parts of oceans worldwide and Mediterranean Sea

**DIET:** Fish (including other sharks), squid, crustaceans, and sometimes seals

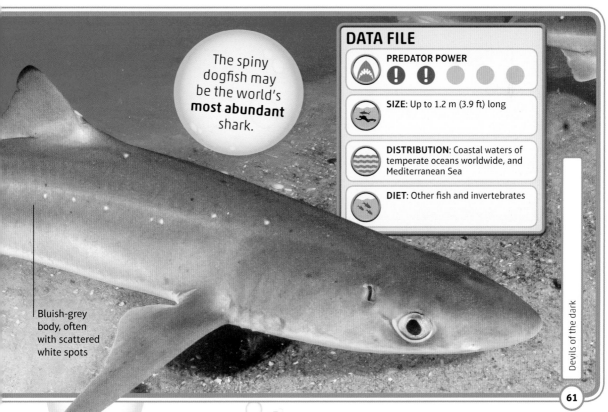

The spiny dogfish may be the world's **most abundant** shark.

## DATA FILE

**PREDATOR POWER** ! !

**SIZE:** Up to 1.2 m (3.9 ft) long

**DISTRIBUTION:** Coastal waters of temperate oceans worldwide, and Mediterranean Sea

**DIET:** Other fish and invertebrates

Bluish-grey body, often with scattered white spots

Devils of the dark

**61**

# PELICAN EEL
*Eurypharynx pelecanoides*

## DATA FILE

**PREDATOR POWER**
 ● ● ● ●

**SIZE:** Up to 1 m (3.3 ft) long

**DISTRIBUTION:** Deep waters of oceans worldwide

**DIET:** Mainly small shrimps and squid

The pelican eel's jaws are seven times longer than its skull's brain case, and its big mouth looks like it tackles giant prey. However, the pelican eel probably uses its enormous jaws to scoop up shoals of shrimps, much like the pelican bird uses the pouch on its giant beak to catch bundles of fish.

Tiny eyes can probably only detect light and movement, without forming a clear image

The pelican eel has one of the **biggest sets of jaws** in proportion to its body size.

Teeth are too small to tackle big fish

Whip-like tail provides propulsion

# SLADEN'S HATCHETFISH

*Argyropelecus sladeni*

Upward-pointing mouth

Its **telescopic eyes** can detect faint light.

Light-producing organs shine downwards to confuse bigger predators swimming below

The tiny, deep-ocean hatchetfish uses clever tactics to be an effective ocean predator. Its bulging eyes are directed upwards so they can spot the shadow of overhead plankton that are small enough to bite. Each night these fish migrate kilometres towards the surface to follow their prey.

## DATA FILE

**PREDATOR POWER**

 **SIZE**: Up to 7 cm (2.8 in) long

 **DISTRIBUTION**: Deep waters of oceans worldwide

 **DIET**: Copepods (small, swimming crustaceans)

Devils of the dark

# BARBELED DRAGONFISH
*Stomias boa*

The barbeled dragonfish has light-producing organs running along its body, and its big scales reflect the light. It gets its name from the long, luminous barbel that projects from its chin – a feature that might help attract the attention of smaller fish, which are then grabbed by a mouth filled with long, pointed teeth.

Light produced by this fish **may confuse bigger predators**.

# SLOANE'S VIPERFISH
*Chauliodus sloani*

**Viperfish, side view**

"Fangs" are so long that it cannot completely close its jaws

When the viperfish attacks, its lower jaw reaches forwards and the top of its head rotates backwards. As a result, its mouth opens to nearly 180 degrees to take a bite. It strikes its victims with such force that it needs specially adapted "neck" vertebrae to absorb the shock of the blow.

Devils of the dark

Large eyes

Hexagonal patches of pigment and light-producing organs line the side of the body

**Barbeled dragonfish, side view**

## DATA FILE

**PREDATOR POWER**

**SIZE**: Up to 32 cm (12.6 in) long

**DISTRIBUTION**: Deep waters of Atlantic and Southern oceans, and Mediterranean Sea

**DIET**: Mainly fish

First dorsal fin ray is long and carries a luminous lure

## DATA FILE

**PREDATOR POWER**

**SIZE**: Up to 35 cm (13.8 in) long

**DISTRIBUTION**: Deep waters of tropical and subtropical oceans

**DIET**: Mainly fish

This fish has the **biggest teeth** in proportion to its body size of all fish.

# DEEP-SEA
# LIZARDFISH
*Bathysaurus ferox*

The deep-sea lizardfish probably spends much of its time on the ocean bottom, rather than swimming in mid-water. Here it probably waits to ambush passing prey, making a grab with strong, alligator-like jaws that extend back beyond its black eyes. Its body is covered with a mosaic of tough scales, like a lizard's scaly skin.

The lizardfish's **barbed teeth** give it **a better grip** on prey.

Wide jaws with needle-like teeth may be strong enough to grab large prey

Skin covered in large, tough scales

**Deep-sea lizardfish, top view**

## DATA FILE

 **PREDATOR POWER**

 **SIZE:** Up to 70 cm (27.6 in) long

**DISTRIBUTION:** Deep waters of oceans worldwide

**DIET:** Fish, squid, crabs, and dead animals drifting down from above

# LANCETFISH

*Alepisaurus* sp.

Sail-like dorsal fin runs along the back of the body

Jaws contain two or three extra-large fangs among the smaller teeth

**Lancetfish, side view**

This has been called the **"cannibal fish"** because it **may eat its own kind**.

Although this fish resembles the speedy sailfish, it lacks the muscle power of that ocean athlete. The unrelated lancetfish relies instead on surprise to catch its prey, so prefers to hunt in deeper, darker water, grabbing anything it can gobble down. Its scientific name, *Alepisaurus*, means "lizard without scales" – a reference to its unusually smooth, somewhat flabby, skin.

## DATA FILE

**PREDATOR POWER**

**SIZE**: Up to 2.1 m (6.9 ft) long

**DISTRIBUTION**: Deep waters of oceans worldwide

**DIET**: Fish, squid, and swimming crustaceans

Devils of the dark

# HUMPBACK
# ANGLERFISH
*Melanocetus johnsonii*

The humpback anglerfish has an extraordinary life history. Only females hunt by using a luminous lure to attract prey within reach of their massive jaws. Males are smaller, and those of some species of deep-sea angler never feed at all. Once a male finds his giant mate, he attaches to her and the pair spawn together.

# GIANT
# SQUID
*Architeuthis dux*

One of the world's biggest animals without a backbone is a little-known giant of the deep sea. Despite its enormous size, and tentacles that can reach longer than a bus, the giant squid is rarely seen. Once caught by the suckers on its tentacles, prey rarely escapes, and is quickly brought to the sharp beak to be dismembered.

Suckers on eight muscular arms and two tentacles help catch prey

Devils of the dark

Light-producing "bulb"

Enormous jaws to grab big prey

The **light in the fish's lure** comes from **bacteria in the lure's "bulb"**.

## DATA FILE

**PREDATOR POWER**

**SIZE**: Females up to 18 cm (7.1 in) long; males up to 2.9 cm (1.1 in) long

**DISTRIBUTION**: Deep-ocean waters worldwide

**DIET**: Fish

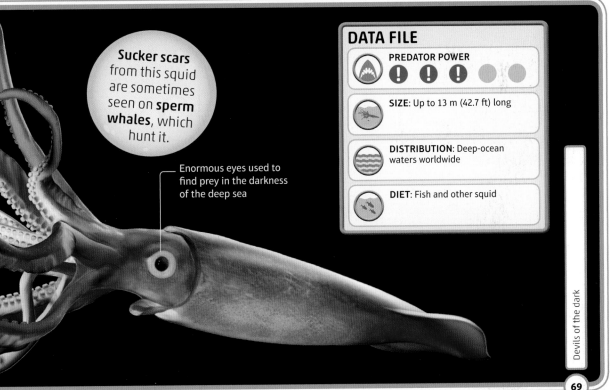

**Sucker scars** from this squid are sometimes seen on **sperm whales**, which hunt it.

Enormous eyes used to find prey in the darkness of the deep sea

## DATA FILE

**PREDATOR POWER**

**SIZE**: Up to 13 m (42.7 ft) long

**DISTRIBUTION**: Deep-ocean waters worldwide

**DIET**: Fish and other squid

Devils of the dark

# VAMPIRE SQUID

*Vampyroteuthis infernalis*

The bizarre vampire squid is only distantly related to "true" squid. Among its unusual features are the thread-like "fishing lines" it uses rather than the tentacles usually found in squid. The vampire squid gets its name from its eyes, which sometimes seem to glow red. However, it is no blood-sucker, and instead preys on small, soft-bodied animals found in plankton.

Webbing connects the eight arms to form a "cloak"

Body covered in light-producing organs that can flash to confuse predators

When threatened, this creature gives off **blobs of blue, glowing mucus**.

## DATA FILE

 **PREDATOR POWER**

 **SIZE**: Up to 30 cm (12 in) long with arms extended

 **DISTRIBUTION**: Deep waters of oceans worldwide

 **DIET**: Planktonic animals, including small crustaceans and jellyfish

# GIANT PACIFIC
# OCTOPUS
*Enteroctopus dofleini*

This octopus can **weigh** as much as **272 kg (600 lb)**.

Eye has a horizontal pupil

Like other octopuses, this species can change colour by expanding tiny sacs of pigment in its skin

Double row of suckers on each of the eight arms grips prey tightly

The giant Pacific octopus grows bigger and lives longer than any other octopus species. An adult female giant Pacific octopus can produce up to 100,000 eggs. A devoted mother, she guards her eggs for five to eight months before they hatch. She also stops hunting, becoming so weak that she dies soon after the eggs hatch.

## DATA FILE

 **PREDATOR POWER**

 **SIZE**: Arm span of up to 9.6 m (31.5 ft)

 **DISTRIBUTION**: Coastal and deep waters of North Pacific Ocean

 **DIET**: Shrimps, crabs, lobsters, clams, scallops, abalones, and fish (including small sharks)

Devils of the dark

# 4

# KILLERS BETWEEN THE TIDES

The coastline, where ocean meets land, is a challenging place to live. Each day the tides drain the shore of water and then flood it completely. However, many kinds of ocean animals can survive out of water during low tide, using rocks and seaweed for shelter. A few sharks even use their fins like legs to waddle between rock pools in search of stranded prey.

# ZEBRA BULLHEAD

*Heterodontus zebra*

Bullhead sharks have very strong jaws for sharks of such small size. They grab crabs, snails, and urchins with sharp, pointed teeth at the front of the jaw and then smash the prey with blunter "cheek" teeth near the back. Many species have bold patterns, and the zebra bullhead is perhaps the most striking of them all.

Brownish, vertical stripes turn black as the shark matures

Cream-coloured body

This fish is popular in **public aquariums**.

## DATA FILE

 **PREDATOR POWER**
 ! !

 **SIZE**: Up to 1.2 m (3.9 ft) long

 **DISTRIBUTION**: Shallow coastal waters of eastern Asia and north-western Australia

 **DIET**: Bottom-living invertebrates

# HORN SHARK

*Heterodontus francisci*

The horn shark gets its name from the horn-like ridges over its eyes. It hunts for invertebrates along rocky shorelines, often using its muscular pectoral fins to clamber over the ocean bottom. Like other bullheads, the female horn shark lays spiral-shaped egg cases, wedging them between rocky crevices as extra protection from predators.

## DATA FILE

 **PREDATOR POWER**

 **SIZE**: Up to 96 cm (37.8 in) long

 **DISTRIBUTION**: Shallow coastal waters of California, Mexico, and probably Ecuador and Peru

 **DIET**: Sea urchins, crabs, shrimps, worms, anemones, molluscs, and small fish

The horn shark has the **strongest bite** of any shark relative to its size.

Body has small, dark spots on a lighter background

Horn-like ridge

# COLLARED
# CARPET SHARK
*Parascyllium collare*

## DATA FILE

 **PREDATOR POWER**
❗ ❗ ⬤ ⬤ ⬤

**SIZE**: Up to 87 cm (34.2 in) long

**DISTRIBUTION**: Shallow coastal waters of eastern Australia

**DIET**: Small, bottom-living fish and invertebrates

Small sharks that live in shallow water are vulnerable to bigger predators, but the markings of the collared carpet shark may help protect it. The markings allow this shark to disguise itself against the background of coral and seaweed. The fish may even alter its colour to match the ocean floor.

Dark spots are scattered over most of the body

Paddle-like pectoral fin lacks spots

This shark lays **long egg cases**.

Like many other related sharks, this species has a dark collar marking the region of the gills

# BLIND SHARK
*Brachaelurus waddi*

The blind shark looks more like a catfish than a shark. It hunts close to the shoreline, and can survive being out of water if stranded in low tide. This small, Australian predator has reasonable vision, but gets its name from its habit of closing its eyelids when danger threatens.

One of two equal-sized dorsal fins

The blind shark can survive for **18 hours** out of water.

Small eye in front of extra-big spiracle, or respiratory opening

Long, sensory barbels help find prey

# ORNATE
# WOBBEGONG
*Orectolobus ornatus*

Wobbegongs are flat-bodied, bottom-living sharks that hunt at night. By day, they rely on the superb camouflage of their intricate colour pattern to stay hidden. The ornate wobbegong likes to rest in underwater caves and under rocky ledges, sometimes in the safety of a large group. Humans that accidentally tread on a wobbegong may get seriously injured by their needle-like teeth.

## DATA FILE

 **PREDATOR POWER**

 **SIZE**: Up to 1.1 m (3.6 ft) long

 **DISTRIBUTION**: Coral reefs and lagoons around New Guinea, and eastern and southern Australia

 **DIET**: Fish (including other sharks), squid, octopuses, and crustaceans

Coloured patches have white spots and crinkled edges

This wobbegong uses its pectoral fins to **"walk"** over rocks.

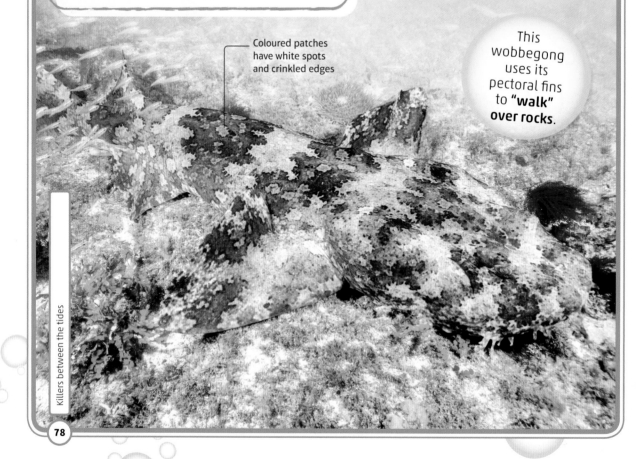

# SPOTTED WOBBEGONG

*Orectolobus maculatus*

Like other wobbegongs, the spotted wobbegong may be seen on the shoreline in shallow water barely deep enough to cover its body. It can even use its strong, flexible pectoral fins like big feet for clambering over rocks from one tidal pool to another. It rests in caves and shipwrecks during the day.

Sharks of this species are known to **rest together, piled up in groups**.

Patchy colour pattern camouflages the shark against the seabed

## DATA FILE

 **PREDATOR POWER**

 **SIZE**: Up to 1.7 m (5.6 ft) long

 **DISTRIBUTION**: Coral reefs and seagrass around Australia

 **DIET**: Fish (including other sharks), crabs, lobsters, and octopuses

Killers between the tides

# COBBLER
# WOBBEGONG
*Sutorectus tentaculatus*

The cobbler wobbegong's body is not as broad and flat as that of other wobbegongs, but it is just as well camouflaged against the Australian sea floor. Its intricate pattern of jigsaw-like skin markings looks so much like the seabed that it is easily overlooked by divers, so little is known about its life.

## DATA FILE

 **PREDATOR POWER**

 **SIZE**: Up to 92 cm (36.2 in) long

 **DISTRIBUTION**: Coral reefs of western and southern Australia

 **DIET**: Bony fish and invertebrates

**Cobbler wobbegong, side view**

Coloured patterns with jagged-edged streaks

# TASSELLED WOBBEGONG
*Eucrossorhinus dasypogon*

This shark can grab prey in a **fraction of a second**.

Of all the strange, bottom-living wobbegongs, the tasselled wobbegong has the best camouflage of them all. Its elaborate tassels look just like fronds of seaweed. This helps it blend well into the coral reef background. With such a perfect disguise, this fish can afford to swim quite slowly, although it can lunge with lightning speed to catch prey with its enormous mouth.

Complicated pattern of lines and spots

"Beard" of branching tassels

## DATA FILE

 **PREDATOR POWER**
❗ ❗ ● ● ●

 **SIZE:** Up to 1.3 m (4.2 ft) long

 **DISTRIBUTION:** Coral reefs of Southeast Asia, New Guinea, and northern Australia

 **DIET:** Bottom-living fish and, possibly, invertebrates

Killers between the tides

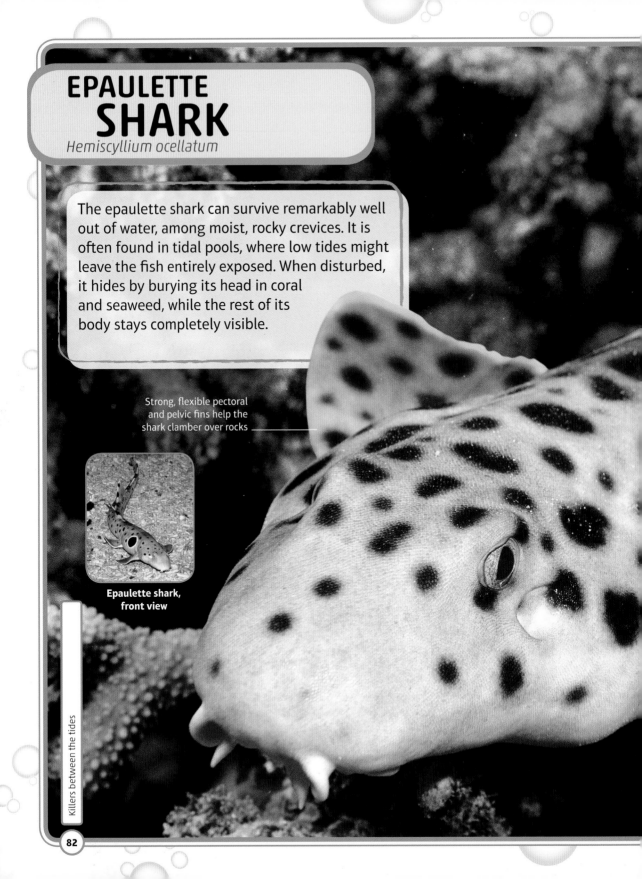

# EPAULETTE
# SHARK
*Hemiscyllium ocellatum*

The epaulette shark can survive remarkably well out of water, among moist, rocky crevices. It is often found in tidal pools, where low tides might leave the fish entirely exposed. When disturbed, it hides by burying its head in coral and seaweed, while the rest of its body stays completely visible.

Strong, flexible pectoral and pelvic fins help the shark clamber over rocks

**Epaulette shark, front view**

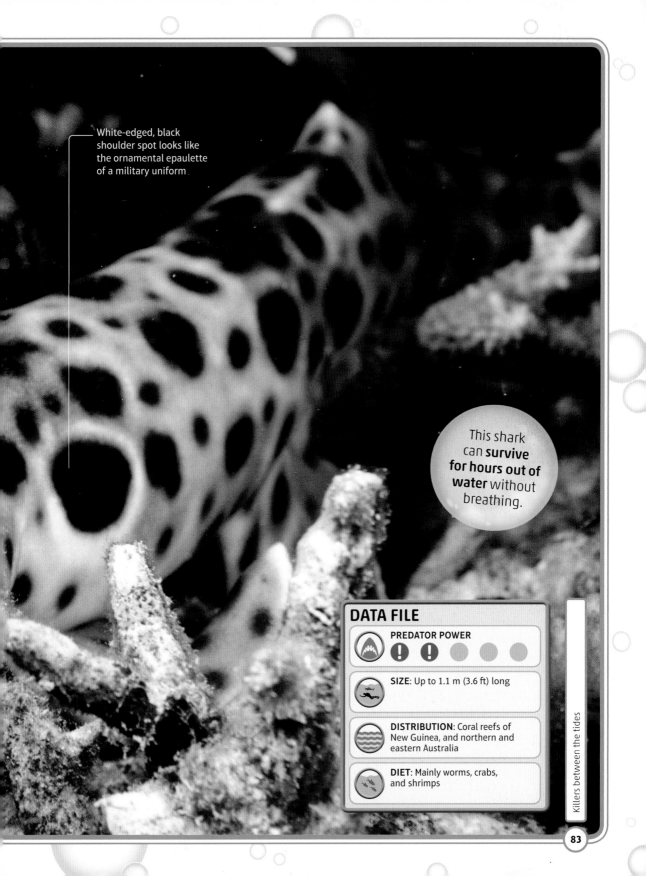

White-edged, black shoulder spot looks like the ornamental epaulette of a military uniform.

This shark can **survive for hours out of water** without breathing.

## DATA FILE

**PREDATOR POWER**

**SIZE**: Up to 1.1 m (3.6 ft) long

**DISTRIBUTION**: Coral reefs of New Guinea, and northern and eastern Australia

**DIET**: Mainly worms, crabs, and shrimps

# WHITE-SPOTTED
## BAMBOOSHARK
*Chiloscyllium plagiosum*

The bambooshark's small, slender body helps it to get between rocky crevices and among coral, either to find shelter from danger or to locate prey. If they get stranded by an ebbing tide, they do not have to worry – some can survive out of water for half a day.

White spots scattered over body

# VENUS
## COMB
*Murex pecten*

Not all snails are harmless herbivores. Members of the whelk family, such as this one, prey on other invertebrates. The Venus comb uses a muscular foot to bore into the shells of other molluscs and barnacles. It then eats the flesh using an extendable body part called a proboscis. The Venus comb gets its name because its shell resembles a hair comb.

Killers between the tides

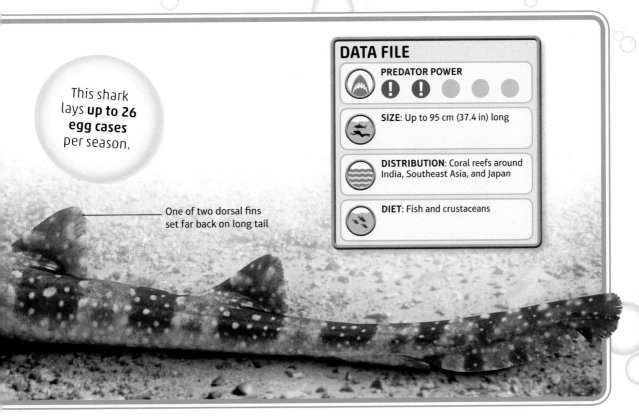

This shark lays **up to 26 egg cases** per season.

One of two dorsal fins set far back on long tail

**DATA FILE**

**PREDATOR POWER**

**SIZE:** Up to 95 cm (37.4 in) long

**DISTRIBUTION:** Coral reefs around India, Southeast Asia, and Japan

**DIET:** Fish and crustaceans

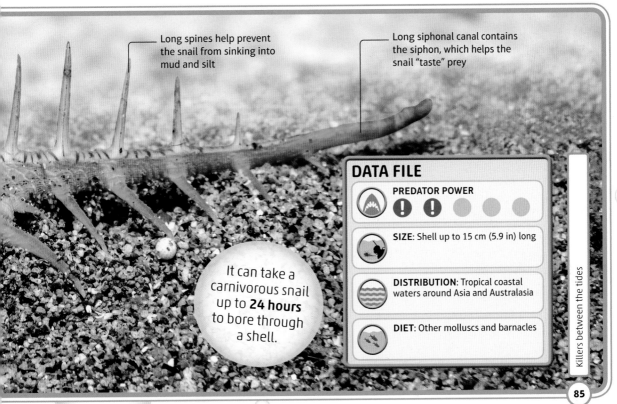

Long spines help prevent the snail from sinking into mud and silt

Long siphonal canal contains the siphon, which helps the snail "taste" prey

It can take a carnivorous snail up to **24 hours** to bore through a shell.

**DATA FILE**

**PREDATOR POWER**

**SIZE:** Shell up to 15 cm (5.9 in) long

**DISTRIBUTION:** Tropical coastal waters around Asia and Australasia

**DIET:** Other molluscs and barnacles

Killers between the tides

# CONE SHELL

*Conus* sp.

Many shell collectors have been badly stung by a cone shell. Its venom is the most potent produced by any kind of snail, and rivals the effects of the ocean's most venomous creatures. The cone shell delivers the venom by projecting a muscular body part called a proboscis, at the tip of which is a rapid-release harpoon that stabs the flesh of the victim.

## DATA FILE

**PREDATOR POWER**

**SIZE:** Shell up to 23 cm (9.1 in) long, depending upon species

**DISTRIBUTION:** Tropical coastal ocean waters worldwide

**DIET:** Fish, worms, and other molluscs

Siphon channels seawater into the snail so it can "taste" the presence of prey

Single, muscular creeping foot helps cone shell glide along

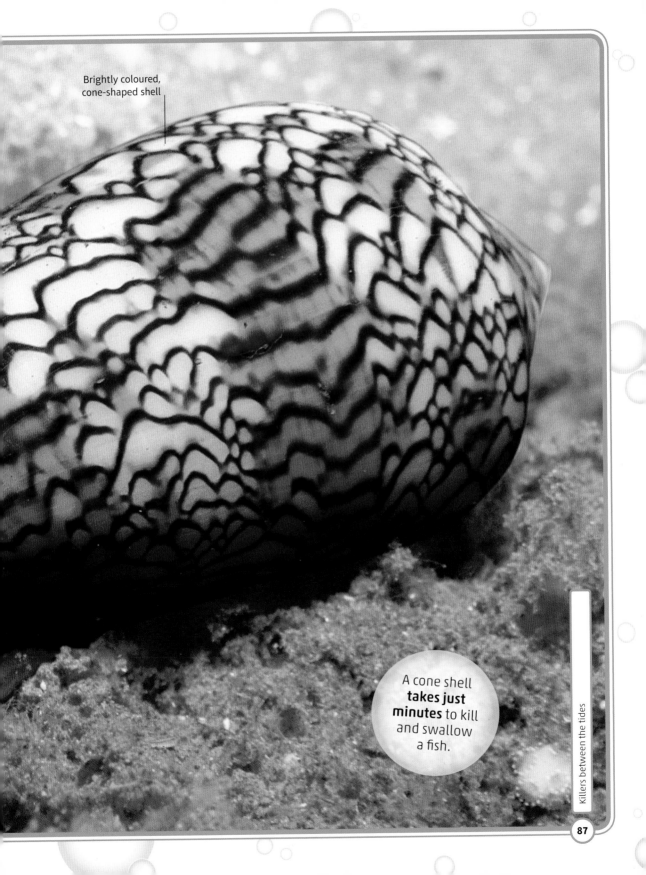

Brightly coloured,
cone-shaped shell

A cone shell
**takes just
minutes** to kill
and swallow
a fish.

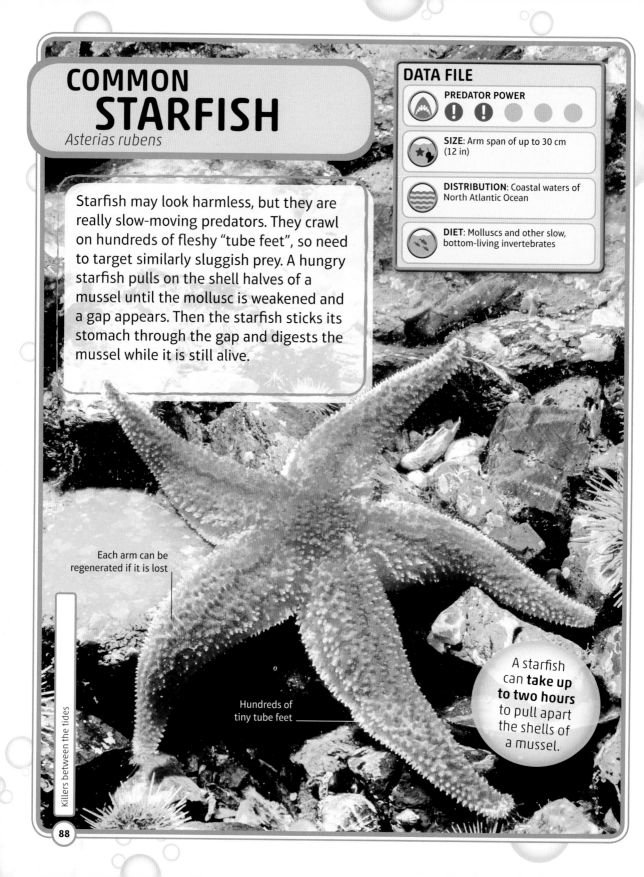

# COMMON
# STARFISH
*Asterias rubens*

Starfish may look harmless, but they are really slow-moving predators. They crawl on hundreds of fleshy "tube feet", so need to target similarly sluggish prey. A hungry starfish pulls on the shell halves of a mussel until the mollusc is weakened and a gap appears. Then the starfish sticks its stomach through the gap and digests the mussel while it is still alive.

## DATA FILE

**PREDATOR POWER**

**SIZE**: Arm span of up to 30 cm (12 in)

**DISTRIBUTION**: Coastal waters of North Atlantic Ocean

**DIET**: Molluscs and other slow, bottom-living invertebrates

Each arm can be regenerated if it is lost

Hundreds of tiny tube feet

A starfish can **take up to two hours** to pull apart the shells of a mussel.

# SOUTHERN BLUE-RINGED
# OCTOPUS
*Hapalochlaena maculosa*

A bite from a blue-ringed octopus could **kill a human in 20 minutes**.

Electric-blue rings

Brown bands along the arms darken when the octopus gets agitated

Octopuses are intelligent hunters. There are many kinds that use bulk and strength to overpower prey, but the tiny blue-ringed octopus uses a powerful venom instead. Its startling electric-blue pattern serves as a warning for bigger animals to stay away. A single bite from this hunter could be fatal for a human.

## DATA FILE

**PREDATOR POWER**
❗ ❗ ❗ ❗ ⬤

**SIZE**: Arm span of up to 20 cm (7.9 in)

**DISTRIBUTION**: Coastal ocean waters off southern Australia

**DIET**: Mainly crustaceans and bivalve molluscs, but sometimes fish

Killers between the tides

# 5
# MUSCLE-
# MOUTHED
# GULPERS

Some sea-living predators have
such a large mouth that prey just
gets sucked inside. These kinds of
hunters can afford to lead a more
sedate lifestyle than the ones
that are speedy enough to lunge.
Some even wait motionless for
prey to come close, until it's gone
in a single, sudden gulp.

# WHALE SHARK

*Rhincodon typus*

Unique, chequerboard pattern of white spots on grey body ⎯

The real giant among sharks grazes gently on plankton, small fish, and squid. The whale shark cruises the sunlit, upper ocean with its enormous mouth open wide to suck in water. Special pads at the back of this shark's mouth strain out tiny animals from the water. The whale shark then swallows these animals down a food pipe that is no wider than a man's arm.

Rough skin, up to 15 cm (6 in) thick in places, is thicker than that of any other animal ⎯⎯⎯

## DATA FILE

 **PREDATOR POWER**

 **SIZE**: Up to 20 m (65.6 ft) long

 **DISTRIBUTION**: Surface waters of tropical and warm temperate oceans worldwide

 **DIET**: Plankton (including krill), small fish, and squid

Small eyes on either side of the enormous mouth

Wide mouth for collecting prey

The whale shark is the **world's biggest living fish.**

# ZEBRA SHARK

*Stegostoma fasciatum*

The zebra shark is a typical suction-feeder, and it captures prey hidden in the sand by hoovering it like a vacuum cleaner. When scientists first studied young zebra sharks, they thought the fish would keep their stripes. That is how these sharks got their name. However, as they grow bigger, their stripes are replaced by spots.

Newborn zebra sharks may **mimic** the appearance of venomous **sea snakes**.

Leopard-like, spotted pattern

Large spiracle (respiratory opening)

# NURSE SHARK

*Ginglymostoma cirratum*

This shark can **suck big snails** out of their shells.

The nurse shark could be the strongest suction-feeding shark of all. By rapidly expanding its throat cavity, it can swallow prey faster than any other shark. When it does this, it makes a slurping sound like a nursing baby, which may be the source of its name.

The mouth looks small, but has very strong suction

Sensory barbels help the shark find prey

## DATA FILE

**PREDATOR POWER**

**SIZE:** Up to 3 m (9.8 ft) long

**DISTRIBUTION:** Shallow coastal waters of tropical Atlantic and eastern Pacific oceans, and Caribbean Sea

**DIET:** Bottom-dwelling invertebrates, bony fish, and sting rays

Strong pectoral fins often help shark to walk on the seabed

**Nurse shark, side view**

Muscle-mouthed gulpers

# TAWNY
# NURSE SHARK
*Nebrius ferrugineus*

This suction-feeder hunts mainly at night, spending the day in the shelter of caves, where several resting sharks may be piled on top of one another. When hunting, the tawny nurse shark can suck fish from between rocks. When caught by anglers, it can spit water in the face of its captor.

Snout is wedge-shaped, with two barbels on the under surface

# ANGLERFISH
*Lophius piscatorius*

The deep-sea anglerfish is a superbly camouflaged seabed predator that has a lure for attracting prey. It waves a little flag on the front of its head, just above its mouth, to attract the attention of a hungry, passing fish. It then uses extendable jaws to snatch its victim in a rapid-action reflex.

Paddle-like pelvic and pectoral fins help the fish "walk" on the ocean floor

Muscle-mouthed gulpers

Dorsal fin is
sharply pointed

This shark often
returns to the
**same resting
spot** each day.

## DATA FILE

**PREDATOR POWER**

**SIZE**: Up to 3.2 m (10.5 ft) long

**DISTRIBUTION**: Tropical coastal
waters of Indian and western Pacific
oceans, and Red Sea

**DIET**: Coral, crabs, lobsters,
octopuses, squid, sea urchins,
and fish

Tail fin makes
up a quarter of
shark's total length

Flag-like appendage
is used to lure prey

Enormous jaws contain
many long, sharp teeth

The anglerfish's
**stomach expands**
to fit in
extra-big prey.

## DATA FILE

**PREDATOR POWER**

**SIZE**: Up to 2 m (6.6 ft) long

**DISTRIBUTION**: Coastal waters of
north-eastern Atlantic Ocean and
Mediterranean Sea

**DIET**: Fish

Leafy fringes on the body help
camouflage the fish on the seabed

Muscle-mouthed gulpers

# PSYCHEDELIC
# FROGFISH
*Histiophryne psychedelica*

Frogfish are the most impressive of the walking anglerfish, having strongly angled fins that serve as feet for waddling along the ocean floor. It lacks the long lure that other anglerfish use to attract prey, and instead relies on its remarkable pattern to blend in with the coral-reef background while waiting to ambush prey.

Exact pattern of white, swirling stripes is unique to each individual

The frilly cheeks may **detect the movement** of predators or prey.

Crawling pectoral fins look like limbs of frogs

Muscle-mouthed gulpers

# PINK FROGMOUTH

*Chaunax pictus*

For ocean predators that are not athletic swimmers, the best tactic is to lie in wait and ambush prey. This balloon-bodied predator belongs to a group of wide-mouthed anglerfish that have sometimes been called sea toads. The pink frogmouth has a lure to attract prey, but also has fleshy fins for "walking" on the ocean floor.

## DATA FILE

**PREDATOR POWER**

**SIZE**: Up to 40 cm (15.7 in) long

**DISTRIBUTION**: Tropical coastal waters of Atlantic Ocean and Mediterranean Sea

**DIET**: Fish and invertebrates

**Tiny, spine-like scales** make this fish's body surface rough.

Short, wiggling lure attracts prey

Squat, leg-like pectoral fins

Golden spots on pink skin

Muscle-mouthed gulpers

# GIANT GROUPER
*Epinephelus lanceolatus*

This enormous fish is one of the top predators – and biggest bony fish – of the tropical reef. It has a voracious appetite and will eat anything that can fit into its mouth, even small sharks. The biggest individuals live out their mostly solitary lives around the vicinity of an underwater cave that is their "lair".

## DATA FILE

 **PREDATOR POWER**

 **SIZE**: Up to 2.7 m (8.9 ft) long

 **DISTRIBUTION**: Tropical coastal waters of Indian and western Pacific oceans

 **DIET**: Mainly crustaceans, but also fish and young sea turtles

Huge fleshy-lipped mouth sucks in prey

Bright patches of colour on juvenile turn dull grey as the fish grows older

Giant groupers **change from female to male** as they mature.

# STONEFISH
*Synanceia verrucosa*

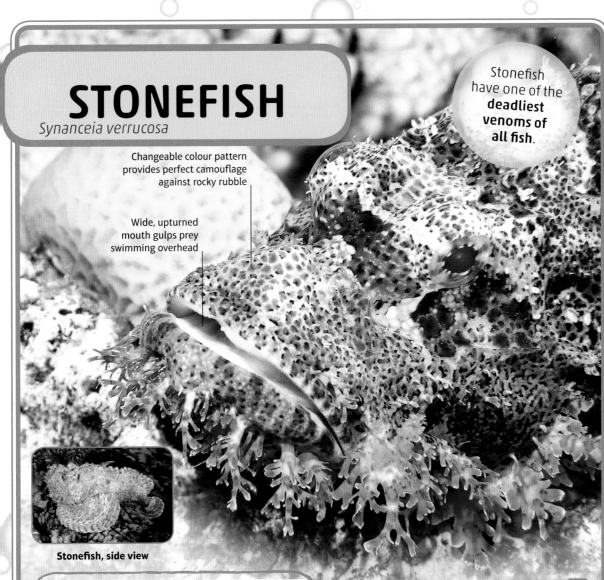

Stonefish have one of the **deadliest venoms of all fish**.

Changeable colour pattern provides perfect camouflage against rocky rubble

Wide, upturned mouth gulps prey swimming overhead

**Stonefish, side view**

The stonefish is a master of camouflage. This big-mouthed predator stays so perfectly disguised among rocks and coral that an unwary snorkeller could easily tread on its venomous spines, resulting in agonizing pain. The fish can survive in the shallowest water in the intertidal zone.

## DATA FILE

**PREDATOR POWER**

**SIZE:** Up to 40 cm (15.7 in) long

**DISTRIBUTION:** Tropical coastal waters of Indian and western Pacific oceans, and Red Sea

**DIET:** Fish and crustaceans

Muscle-mouthed gulpers

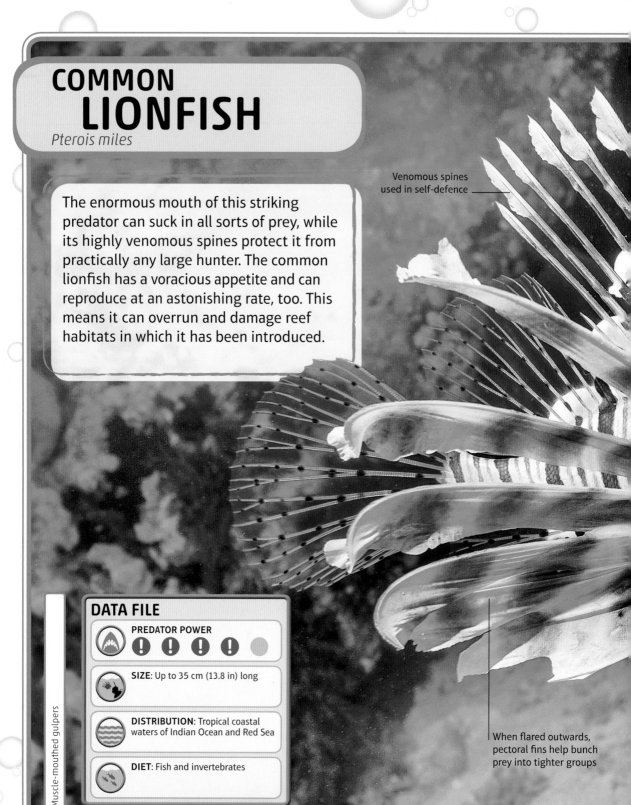

# COMMON
# LIONFISH
*Pterois miles*

The enormous mouth of this striking predator can suck in all sorts of prey, while its highly venomous spines protect it from practically any large hunter. The common lionfish has a voracious appetite and can reproduce at an astonishing rate, too. This means it can overrun and damage reef habitats in which it has been introduced.

Venomous spines used in self-defence

When flared outwards, pectoral fins help bunch prey into tighter groups

## DATA FILE

**PREDATOR POWER**

**SIZE:** Up to 35 cm (13.8 in) long

**DISTRIBUTION:** Tropical coastal waters of Indian Ocean and Red Sea

**DIET:** Fish and invertebrates

This predator's stomach can grow **30 times larger** when filling up with prey.

Large, shovel-shaped mouth can swallow big prey

Stripy pattern helps break up the outline of the lionfish

# 6
# CRUISERS AND CHASERS

In the open ocean, the food chain starts near the surface, with tiny algae and animals (called plankton) drifting by in their billions. Some giants, such as manta rays, feed on this plankton; others chase meatier prey. Some bony fish, such as the sailfish, even have internal heating that makes them very speedy.

# BASKING SHARK
*Cetorhinus maximus*

The basking shark has a sedate lifestyle. This giant cruises the ocean's waters with its mouth gaping to filter planktonic food. Unlike the bigger whale shark, this fish does not gulp water, but takes in water like a giant funnel; enough to fill two Olympic-sized swimming pools every hour.

Enormous gill slits almost completely encircle the head

The largest basking sharks can **weigh over 3 tonnes**.

## DATA FILE

 **PREDATOR POWER**
❗ ● ● ● ●

 **SIZE**: Up to 10 m (33 ft) long

 **DISTRIBUTION**: Oceans worldwide outside the tropics, and Mediterranean Sea

 **DIET**: Shrimps, fish eggs, small fish, and other planktonic animals

Small eyes at
the base of
conical snout

Cavernous mouth
funnels plankton-rich
water over the gills

# MEGAMOUTH SHARK

*Megachasma pelagios*

When scientists found the first megamouth shark in 1976, they decided it was unusual and classified it in a new family on its own. This giant is a filter-feeder and a slow swimmer, but it makes up for it by an impressive vertical migration. It follows plankton into deep waters by day, and rises to the surface at night.

## DATA FILE

 **PREDATOR POWER**

 **SIZE**: Up to 5.5 m (18 ft) long

 **DISTRIBUTION**: Found in patches of open ocean worldwide

 **DIET**: Mainly shrimps of the ocean's plankton, small fish, and jellyfish

There have been only about **60 sightings** of the megamouth.

Flabby body contains an oil-rich liver that makes the fish more buoyant in water

**Megamouth shark, side view**

Wide mouth opens to funnel seawater over the gills, where plankton is filtered out and swallowed

# SMALL-TOOTHED
# SANDTIGER SHARK
*Odontaspis ferox*

Although the small-toothed sandtiger often swims in open water over the deep ocean, it regularly patrols rocky reefs, drop-offs, and gullies. Like its close relatives, it is an active hunter. This shark has slightly bigger eyes than the sandtiger shark, suggesting it is more used to searching for prey in darker waters.

Greyish body helps to distinguish this shark from the browner sandtiger shark

Long teeth give the mouth a "toothy" appearance

## DATA FILE

 **PREDATOR POWER**

 **SIZE:** Up to 4.5 m (14.7 ft) long

 **DISTRIBUTION:** Coastal and deep waters of oceans worldwide and Mediterranean Sea

 **DIET:** Fish, squid, and shrimps

This shark is also known as the **bumpytail ragged-tooth**.

Cruisers and chasers

# SANDTIGER SHARK

*Carcharias taurus*

Slightly flattened, conical snout

Long, slender teeth give the shark a "toothy" appearance

The sandtiger shark **gulps air** for extra **buoyancy**.

The sandtiger shark has one of the biggest brains of related shark species, making it a clever hunter. Groups of sandtiger shark may work together to "herd" shoals of fish, often coming near coastlines and over reefs to do so. These predators have a complex courtship too, and males even guard females after mating.

## DATA FILE

**PREDATOR POWER**

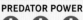 **SIZE**: Up to 3.2 m (10.5 ft) long

 **DISTRIBUTION**: Coastal waters of warm, temperate and tropical oceans, and Mediterranean Sea

 **DIET**: Fish and invertebrates

Cruisers and chasers

# CROCODILE SHARK
*Pseudocarcharias kamoharai*

Crocodile sharks may **migrate to the surface** at night, perhaps trailing prey.

Large eyes

Like most sharks, lower jaw projects forward (is "extensible") to help shark grab prey easily

**Crocodile shark, side view**

This small, swift-moving hunter spends its days in deep water, so is rarely seen. The crocodile shark uses its big eyes to hunt in near darkness. Like some other related sharks, it has a small litter size, but stronger youngsters may eat their weaker siblings while they are still inside their mother's womb.

## DATA FILE

**PREDATOR POWER**

**SIZE**: Up to 1.2 m (3.9 ft) long

**DISTRIBUTION**: Deep ocean waters of tropical oceans worldwide

**DIET**: Fish, squid, and shrimps

# GREAT
## WHITE SHARK
*Carcharodon carcharias*

The great white shark probably has the strongest bite of any living animal. It usually lives in the upper layers of the open ocean, but often comes near the shore in search of prey. Younger great whites hunt for fish. As these sharks grow bigger, they turn to more warm-blooded prey, and are drawn to places where seals are abundant along the shoreline.

Long slits help the gills extract plenty of oxygen from water

Great whites can detect a **drop of blood** from **5 km (3 miles) away**.

**Great white shark, side view**

Massive, strong jaws can easily grab ocean mammals, such as seals and large fish

White underside contrasts sharply with grey upper body

## DATA FILE

**PREDATOR POWER**

**SIZE:** Up to 6 m (19.7 ft) long

**DISTRIBUTION:** Open coastal waters in oceans worldwide

**DIET:** Seals, dolphins, turtles, seabirds, and large fish

# SHORT-FINNED MAKO
*Isurus oxyrinchus*

Blue or purplish colour helps disguise the mako shark against the background of the open ocean

Streamlined shape helps this shark move faster in the water

A mako is known to have covered **13,000 km (8,077 miles)** in six months.

The muscular mako shark shoots through water in bursts of speed that can reach 100 kph (60 mph), making it a champion hunter of the open ocean and the fastest shark of all. Sometimes mako sharks will even jump right out of the water. They make extraordinary migrations too, crossing huge stretches of ocean at a time.

## DATA FILE

 **PREDATOR POWER**

 **SIZE:** Up to 4 m (13.1 ft) long

 **DISTRIBUTION:** Open and coastal waters of oceans worldwide and Mediterranean Sea

 **DIET:** Mainly fish and squid; larger sharks hunt small dolphins

# SALMON
# SHARK
*Lamna ditropis*

## DATA FILE

 **PREDATOR POWER**
❗ ❗ ❗ ● ●

 **SIZE**: Up to 3 m (9.8 ft) long

 **DISTRIBUTION**: Open and coastal waters of North Pacific Ocean

 **DIET**: Schooling fish, such as salmon and herrings

The high body temperature of this warm-blooded shark helps it stay active even when it is in cold water. This means its range can extend right into the chilly extremes of the far northern Pacific, where it can keep hunting in water too cold for many other sharks. The salmon shark hunts in groups to chase schools of fish, following the migrations of prey.

This shark is known to **hunt in groups** of 30 or 40.

Dusky blotches on paler underside of body

Long gill slits help the shark get plenty of oxygen from water

Cruisers and chasers

# THRESHER SHARK

*Alopias vulpinus*

## DATA FILE

 **PREDATOR POWER**
❗ ❗ ❗ ● ●

 **SIZE**: Up to 5.8 m (19 ft)

 **DISTRIBUTION**: Coastal and open-ocean waters worldwide

 **DIET**: Small fish, such as anchovies and mackerel, and squid, octopuses, and crustaceans

Few ocean animals can match the athleticism of the thresher shark. It chases prey just below the surface of the open ocean and has an astonishing technique for subduing targets. It uses the strap-like upper lobe of its tail, which grows the length of its body, to whip the water, stunning small fish so they can be easily gobbled up.

Extra-long upper lobe of tail

White patch extending above the pectoral fin identifies this species from other threshers

The **speed of this shark's tail** whip can be up to **130 kph (80.7 mph)**.

Narrow, sickle-shaped pectoral fins

# GOBLIN SHARK

*Mitsukurina owstoni*

Long, flat snout packed with sensors that detect prey

Small eyes suggest vision is poor

A soft body suggests the goblin shark **swims mid-water**.

Nail-like teeth

Flabby skin

Goblin shark, side view

One of the most bizarre of all sharks, the goblin shark is a ghostly pale pink. Its body is so soft and flabby that it is probably not a strong swimmer. To find prey, it sweeps the water with its long, sensitive snout. Then it shoots out extensible jaws to snap at any prey within reach.

## DATA FILE

**PREDATOR POWER**

**SIZE**: Up to 3.8 m (12.5 ft) long

**DISTRIBUTION**: Open oceans worldwide

**DIET**: Probably deep-water, soft-bodied fish and squid

Cruisers and chasers

# SPOTTED EAGLE RAY

*Aetobatus narinari*

Tail may have 2–6 venomous spines

Enormous pectoral fins flap to make the ray "fly" through water

Eagle rays often **perform acrobatics** by jumping out of the water.

Shovel-like lower jaw digs for prey in sand

This close relative of the manta ray shares its cousin's habit of swimming in open water. However, unlike the manta, the spotted eagle ray does not feed on plankton. Instead, it hunts for bottom-living prey. Its strong jaws can crunch through a crab's hard shell.

## DATA FILE

 **PREDATOR POWER**

 **SIZE:** Up to 5 m (16.4 ft) long and 3.3 m (10.8 ft) wide

 **DISTRIBUTION:** Tropical coastal waters of western Atlantic, Indian, and Pacific oceans

 **DIET:** Molluscs, crabs, octopuses, small fish, and worms

# GIANT MANTA RAY

*Manta birostris*

This giant among rays cruises the open ocean with graceful flaps of its "wings". Unlike most other rays, which are bottom-living, the manta ray is a swimming filter-feeder. It funnels plankton-rich water into its enormous mouth with the help of its horn-like cephalic fins. Special spongy structures on its gills then strain out the food.

**Giant manta ray, top view**

Horn-like cephalic fins curve round to funnel plankton-rich water into mouth ——————

## DATA FILE

**PREDATOR POWER**

**SIZE**: Up to 4.5 m (14.8 ft) long and 9 m (29.5 ft) wide

**DISTRIBUTION**: Tropical and subtropical open-ocean waters worldwide

**DIET**: Shrimps, krill, and other small planktonic animals

The giant manta ray is the **world's biggest species of ray**.

# GREAT BARRACUDA
*Sphyraena barracuda*

Barracudas have long, pointed jaws and fang-like teeth that are not only perfect for grabbing small prey, but also good for ripping off lumps of flesh from bigger animals. Smaller barracudas hunt together in shoals in the open ocean, but the biggest ones live alone and have even been known to injure human divers.

## DATA FILE

 **PREDATOR POWER**
   ! ! !

 **SIZE:** Up to at least 2 m (6.6 ft) long

 **DISTRIBUTION:** Tropical and subtropical open ocean worldwide

**DIET:** Fish, cephalopods, and occasionally shrimps

One of two widely separated dorsal fins

Pike-like jaws and dagger-like teeth

Barracudas can attack with bursts of **speed up to 58 kph (36 mph)**.

Cruisers and chasers

120

# SAILFISH
*Istiophorus albicans*

Long, sword-like bill

Sail is raised to scare prey into tighter shoals, but lowered for high-speed chases

A fast-moving hunter of the open ocean, the sailfish is perfectly equipped for high-speed chases. As well as having a streamlined body that can cut through water easily, it stores extra oxygen in its red muscles. It can even generate heat in its head, which helps it keep its brain and eyes working efficiently.

## DATA FILE

 **PREDATOR POWER**

 **SIZE**: Up to 3.2 m (10.5 ft) long

 **DISTRIBUTION**: Tropical and subtropical open ocean worldwide

 **DIET**: Fish and squid

The sailfish is the **world's fastest** fish. It can reach speeds up to 110 kph (68 mph).

# ATLANTIC
# BLUEFIN TUNA
*Thunnus thynnus*

Tuna can swim at **speeds of 72.4 kph (45 mph)**.

Bright yellow "finlets" between second dorsal fin and tail

Metallic blue above, silver white below

The Atlantic bluefin tuna generates more body heat than almost any other kind of fish. This trait, along with the high oxygen-carrying capacity of its blood, makes it one of the speediest athletes in the ocean. The power for swimming comes from its flicking tail, while its body stays rigid to create a sleeker shape that cuts through the water with ease.

## DATA FILE

 **PREDATOR POWER**

 **SIZE**: Up to 4.6 m (15.1 ft) long

 **DISTRIBUTION**: Open waters of Atlantic Ocean and Mediterranean Sea

 **DIET**: Squid, fish, and crustaceans

# GIANT TREVALLY
*Caranx ignobilis*

This fish belongs to a family that is related to the sailfish and other open-ocean athletes, but the giant trevally sticks closer to coastal reefs. Juveniles even enter rivers and estuaries. The fish hunts alone or in groups. Individuals sometimes ambush their prey by hiding in the cover of big sharks.

This fish sometimes follows hunting seals to **steal their prey**.

Prominent, high forehead

Keels along the side of the body help increase swimming speed

Cruisers and chasers

**123**

# HUMPBACK
# WHALE
## *Megaptera novaeangliae*

Particularly long pectoral flippers help make this species the most acrobatic of giant whales

The humpback's song is the **loudest and most complex** of any whale.

Despite its size, the humpback whale is one of the most agile of whale species. Its giant flippers are bigger than those of any other animal, and help it make sharp turns in the water for bunching shoals of fish and shrimps. It even blows a screen of bubbles from its blowhole to prevent their escape.

Grooves and elasticated skin
allow expansion of throat
to take in huge volume of
water containing prey

## DATA FILE

**PREDATOR POWER**

**SIZE:** Up to 11.9 m (39 ft) long

**DISTRIBUTION:** Open ocean
worldwide

**DIET:** Small fish and krill

Cruisers and chasers

# SPERM WHALE
*Physeter macrocephalus*

Barrel-like spermaceti organ in head is filled with oil and used for generating sound

Only the lower jaw contains teeth

The sperm whale is the **world's biggest toothed predator**.

The sperm whale is a record-breaker: it has the biggest brain of any animal and can dive to depths that rival the achievements of most other diving mammals. It specializes in hunting deep-sea squid, but, like all whales, must periodically come to the surface to breathe air.

## DATA FILE

**PREDATOR POWER**

**SIZE**: Up to 19.2 m (63 ft) long

**DISTRIBUTION**: Open-ocean waters worldwide

**DIET**: Mainly squid

# LEATHERBACK
# TURTLE
*Dermochelys coriacea*

The leatherback turtle can travel more than 60 km (37.3 miles) in a day, with scarcely any rest during this time. Most reptiles are cold-blooded, so they are not very active in cold conditions, but this turtle can generate so much body heat it can even keep hunting in cold waters approaching the Arctic Circle.

This is the world's **biggest species of turtle**.

Leathery skin instead of hard-plated shell

Enormous flippers make turtle a powerful swimmer

## DATA FILE

 **PREDATOR POWER**
 **SIZE:** Usually up to 1.8 m (5.9 ft) long

 **DISTRIBUTION:** Open-ocean waters worldwide

 **DIET:** Almost entirely jellyfish, but sometimes squid and other soft-bodied animals

Cruisers and chasers

# BOX
# JELLYFISH

*Chironex* sp.

Cube-shaped bell

Human swimmers fear the box jellyfish more than any other because of its terrible sting. Large swarms may gather during warmer months, often near the shore. This creature uses eyes to help find food. Its long tentacles can catch fish, paralysing them with powerful venom.

Long tentacles have thousands of stingers

Unlike other jellyfish, this one's **bell has eyes** to sense light and movement.

## DATA FILE

**PREDATOR POWER**

**SIZE**: Bell up to 30 cm (11.8 in) wide; tentacles up to 3 m (9.8 ft) long when fully extended

**DISTRIBUTION**: Tropical and subtropical open-ocean waters worldwide

**DIET**: Fish and other small planktonic animals

# LION'S MANE
# JELLYFISH
*Cyanea capillata*

Massive bell pulsates to propel the animal through water

This giant among jellyfish can weigh up to a tonne. It is a cold-water animal, preferring to stay close to Arctic ice, although individuals may drift long distances, and sometimes wash ashore in other parts of the world. Swarms of this jellyfish occasionally gather in the open ocean.

This is the world's **biggest species** of jellyfish.

Tight cluster of more than one thousand tentacles resembles a lion's mane

## DATA FILE

**PREDATOR POWER**

**SIZE:** Bell up to 2.3 m (7.5 ft) wide; tentacles up to 37 m (121.4 ft) long when fully extended

**DISTRIBUTION:** Cold open-ocean waters of North Atlantic and North Pacific oceans

**DIET:** Fish and other jellyfish

Cruisers and chasers

# PORTUGUESE MAN O' WAR

*Physalia physalis*

Gas-filled float catches ocean breezes, like a sail _____

Although it looks like a jellyfish, the Portuguese Man o' War is a colony of tentacle-like animals hanging from a balloon-like float. The longest tentacles are muscular stingers that grab prey. Other structures have mouths for swallowing paralysed fish, or organs for producing eggs.

## DATA FILE

 **PREDATOR POWER**
❗ ❗ ❗ ❗ ⬤

 **SIZE:** Float up to 30 cm (11.8 in) long; tentacles up to 50 m (164 ft) long when fully extended

 **DISTRIBUTION:** Tropical and subtropical open-ocean waters worldwide

 **DIET:** Fish and other invertebrates

Parts of the colony – called zooids – hang in tentacles from the float _____

The colony can **deflate its float** to submerge briefly.

# BARREL SHRIMP

*Phronima* sp.

The barrel shrimp has a grotesque life history. It gets its name because the female preys on floating "jellies", scooping out their insides and using the barrel-shaped husk as a brooding chamber for her eggs. She pushes the barrel around with her, like a pram, until the eggs hatch.

Husk of dead salp used as brooding chamber

Large head has strong biting mouthparts

This predator has inspired **monster movies**.

Cruisers and chasers

# 7

# INSHORE MARAUDERS

Predators that hunt close to land often have rich sources of food. Nutrients from the land can make underwater forests of seaweed and coral thrive in the sunlit shallows. A group of sharks, called the requiem sharks, dominate the inshore marauders. Many are expert at striking prey, unseen, in waters clouded by churned up silt and mud around the margins of landmasses.

# AUSTRALIAN SWELL SHARK
*Cephaloscyllium laticeps*

One of several kinds of swell shark that are found in warm regions throughout the world, the Australian swell shark inflates its stomach by gulping in water when danger threatens. This helps to wedge it inside rocky crevices, so a predator cannot pull it free.

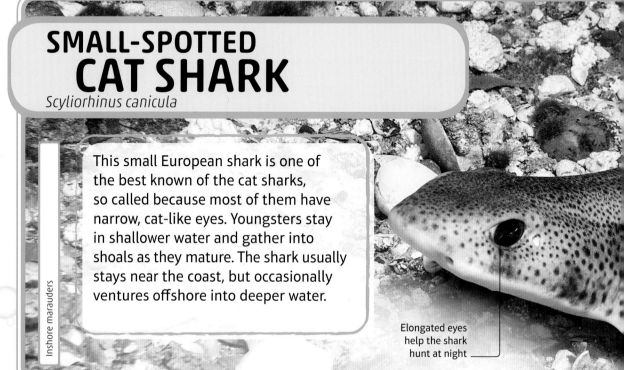

# SMALL-SPOTTED CAT SHARK
*Scyliorhinus canicula*

This small European shark is one of the best known of the cat sharks, so called because most of them have narrow, cat-like eyes. Youngsters stay in shallower water and gather into shoals as they mature. The shark usually stays near the coast, but occasionally ventures offshore into deeper water.

Elongated eyes help the shark hunt at night

Inshore marauders

Colour pattern composed of brownish-grey saddles and blotches

Brow ridges may protect this shark's eyes when it **hides among rocks**.

## DATA FILE

**PREDATOR POWER**

**SIZE:** Up to 1.5 m (4.9 ft) long

**DISTRIBUTION:** Coastal waters around southern Australia and Tasmania

**DIET:** Small fish, crustaceans, and squid

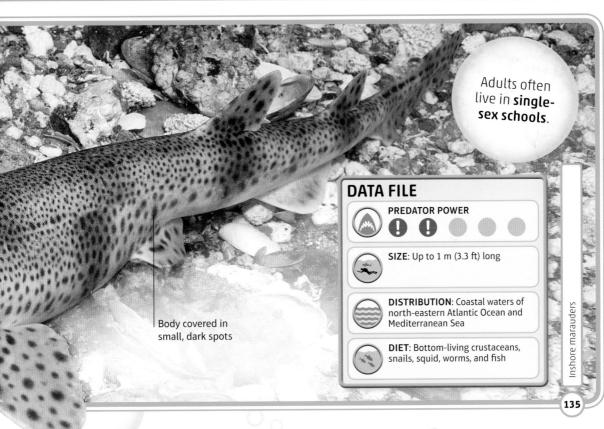

Adults often live in **single-sex schools**.

Body covered in small, dark spots

## DATA FILE

**PREDATOR POWER**

**SIZE:** Up to 1 m (3.3 ft) long

**DISTRIBUTION:** Coastal waters of north-eastern Atlantic Ocean and Mediterranean Sea

**DIET:** Bottom-living crustaceans, snails, squid, worms, and fish

Inshore marauders

# CORAL CAT SHARK

*Atelomycterus marmoratus*

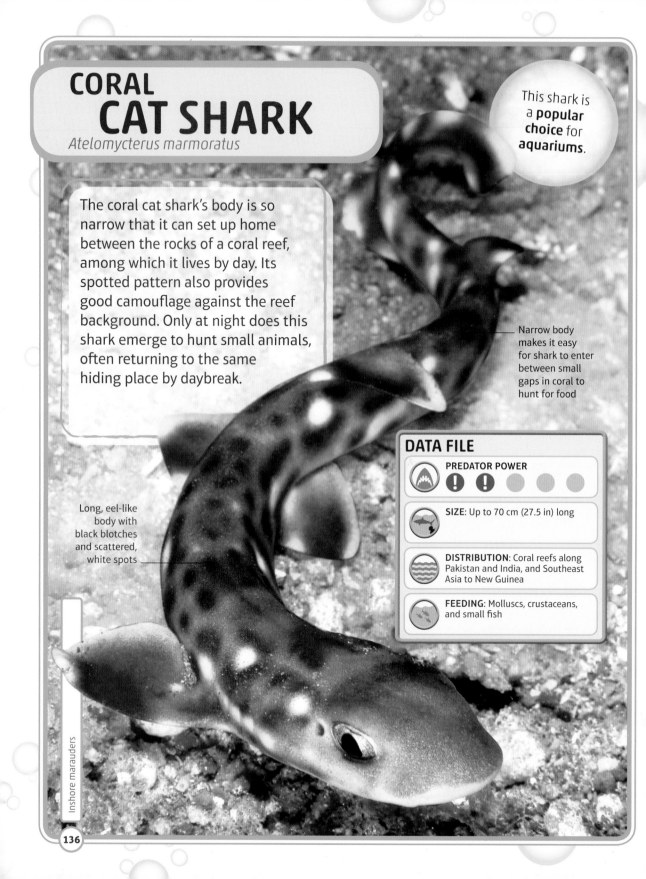

This shark is a **popular choice** for **aquariums**.

The coral cat shark's body is so narrow that it can set up home between the rocks of a coral reef, among which it lives by day. Its spotted pattern also provides good camouflage against the reef background. Only at night does this shark emerge to hunt small animals, often returning to the same hiding place by daybreak.

Narrow body makes it easy for shark to enter between small gaps in coral to hunt for food

Long, eel-like body with black blotches and scattered, white spots

## DATA FILE

**PREDATOR POWER**
! !

**SIZE**: Up to 70 cm (27.5 in) long

**DISTRIBUTION**: Coral reefs along Pakistan and India, and Southeast Asia to New Guinea

**FEEDING**: Molluscs, crustaceans, and small fish

Inshore marauders

# PYJAMA SHARK
*Poroderma africanum*

No other shark has the stripy, pyjama-like costume of this little hunter. Like most other cat sharks, the pyjama shark is a nocturnal hunter, active at night. It prefers rocky areas in which there are plenty of caves for shelter, but it may sometimes venture into very shallow water in the seashore's intertidal zone (the area under water at high tide).

## DATA FILE

**PREDATOR POWER**

**SIZE:** Up to 1 m (3.3 ft) long

**DISTRIBUTION:** Shallow coastal waters of South Africa

**FEEDING:** Fish and invertebrates

Dark stripes run down the length of the body

This shark can **tear tentacles** from a small octopus.

Narrow eyes are higher on the head than in many other cat sharks

Inshore marauders

# RED-SPOTTED CAT SHARK
*Schroederichthys chilensis*

Like many other kinds of cat shark, the red-spotted cat shark from South America has a blotchy skin pattern. At times the blotches intensify and can break up the outline of the fish, especially against the background of the kelp (seaweed) fronds found in its shoreline habitat. Despite its name, the spots on its skin are brown, rather than red.

Dark "saddles" at intervals along the body

Dark brown spots outnumber white spots

This shark can **stay absolutely still** when picked up by divers.

## DATA FILE

 **PREDATOR POWER**
❗ ❗ ● ● ●

 **SIZE**: Up to 70 cm (27.6 in) long

 **DISTRIBUTION**: Shallow coastal waters along the Pacific coast of Peru and Chile

 **DIET**: Small crustaceans and other invertebrates

# PUFFADDER SHY SHARK

*Haploblepharus edwardsii*

Shy sharks form a group of small, mainly brightly patterned, sharks from South Africa that get their name from an extraordinary response to danger. When threatened, they curl up into a ring and cover their eyes with their tail. The puffadder shy shark lives on sandy or rocky bottoms, usually close to the shore, and often in groups.

The **curled-up posture** may stop bigger sharks from taking a bite.

Golden-brown "saddles" with darker margins

Small, white blotches scattered across body

## DATA FILE

 **PREDATOR POWER**

 **SIZE:** Up to 60 cm (23.6 in) long

 **HABITAT:** Shallow coastal waters of South Africa

 **DIET:** Fish, crustaceans, squid, and worms

Inshore marauders

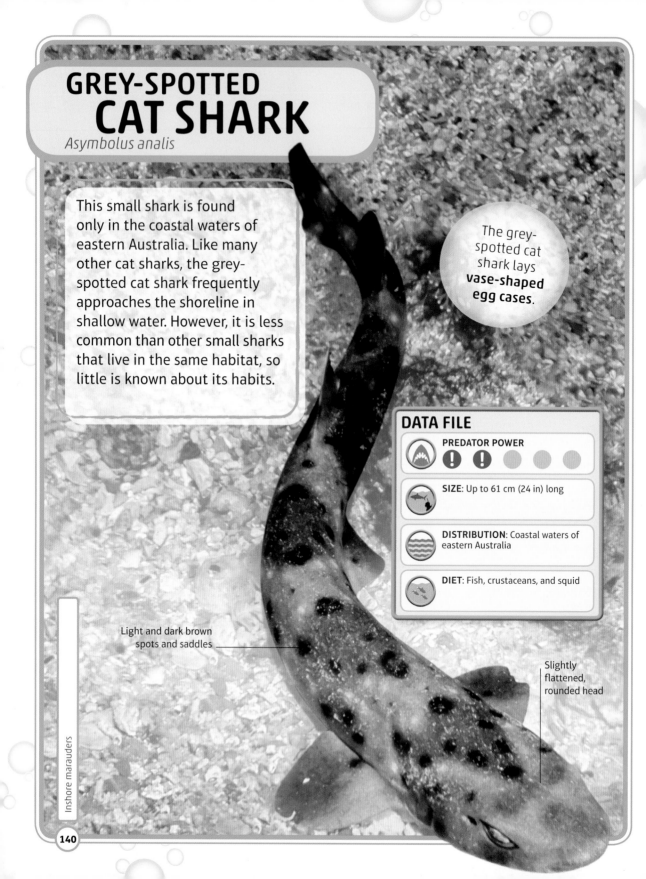

# GREY-SPOTTED
# CAT SHARK
*Asymbolus analis*

This small shark is found only in the coastal waters of eastern Australia. Like many other cat sharks, the grey-spotted cat shark frequently approaches the shoreline in shallow water. However, it is less common than other small sharks that live in the same habitat, so little is known about its habits.

The grey-spotted cat shark lays **vase-shaped egg cases**.

## DATA FILE

**PREDATOR POWER**

**SIZE**: Up to 61 cm (24 in) long

**DISTRIBUTION**: Coastal waters of eastern Australia

**DIET**: Fish, crustaceans, and squid

Light and dark brown spots and saddles

Slightly flattened, rounded head

# BLACK-MOUTHED CAT SHARK

*Galeus melastomus*

The black-mouthed cat shark lives in deeper water than many cat sharks, swimming in the ocean where the continental shelf drops sharply towards the abyss. Here, its sensitive vision can follow the glow of animals, such as the lanternfish. This shark sticks close to the bottom and uses its long body to swim with slow, eel-like undulations.

Large eyes

Dark saddles, blotches, and circular spots run the length of the body

Female black-mouthed cat sharks lay up to **100 egg cases** each year.

## DATA FILE

 **PREDATOR POWER**

 **SIZE:** Up to 90 cm (35.4 in) long

 **DISTRIBUTION:** Coastal waters of northeastern Atlantic Ocean, North Sea, and Mediterranean Sea

 **DIET:** Lanternfish and bottom-living invertebrates, such as shrimps and squid

# BIG-EYED
## HOUND SHARK
*Iago omanensis*

The extra-long gill slits of the big-eyed hound shark may help it survive in warm waters, in which oxygen levels are too low to support other kinds of shark. This fish can also tolerate higher salt concentrations than other sharks. It lives in the Red Sea, and a related species lives in the Bay of Bengal.

Gills inside these long slits can extract plenty of oxygen

Large, green eyes help this shark hunt in dark water

# TOPE
## SHARK
*Galeorhinus galeus*

A tope shark has migrated a record distance of **2,525 km** (**1,569 miles**).

Topes are closely related to inshore reef sharks, but wander much further out to sea. The common tope's urge to migrate sees it travel long distances regularly. These sharks prefer lower sea temperatures. They either move away from the equator during the warmest months, or go into deeper, cooler waters.

Inshore marauders

The males live in **deeper waters** than the females.

## DATA FILE

**PREDATOR POWER**

**SIZE:** Up to 58 cm (22.8 in) long

**DISTRIBUTION:** Warm coastal waters of Red Sea, Gulf of Oman, and possibly Bay of Bengal

**DIET:** Fish, squid, and octopuses

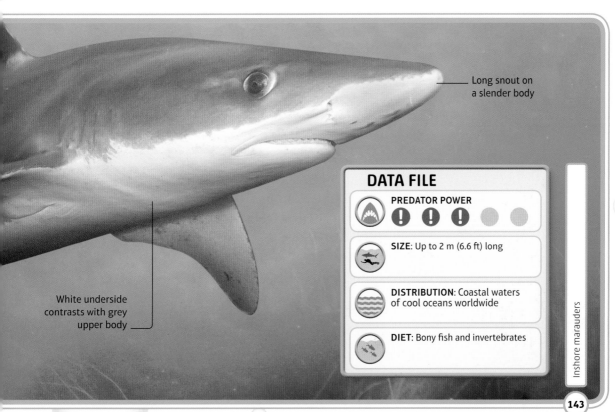

Long snout on a slender body

White underside contrasts with grey upper body

## DATA FILE

**PREDATOR POWER**

**SIZE:** Up to 2 m (6.6 ft) long

**DISTRIBUTION:** Coastal waters of cool oceans worldwide

**DIET:** Bony fish and invertebrates

Inshore marauders

# LEOPARD SHARK
*Triakis semifasciata*

Leopard sharks **can tear a clam** from **its shell**.

Centre of each dark, saddle-like marking gets paler as the shark matures

Broad, rounded snout

This strikingly patterned North American shark lives in shallow waters with low oxygen levels, such as around bays and estuaries. The leopard shark likes to follow the ebb and flow of the tide in search of mud-living prey and is often seen in the company of other similar-sized sharks. Females venture into eelgrass beds in water less than a metre deep to give birth.

## DATA FILE

**PREDATOR POWER**

**SIZE**: Up to 1.8 m (5.9 ft) long

**DISTRIBUTION**: Shallow coastal waters and estuaries along the Pacific coast of North America

**DIET**: Crabs, clams, worms, and fish

# STARRY SMOOTH HOUND

*Mustelus asterias*

The starry smooth hound gets its name from the small, white, star-like spots on its body, although, in many cases, these markings may be faint. It swims over sand and gravel, and migrates further inshore during summer months. Like its close relatives, this shark uses its crushing jaws and teeth to feed on crabs and other crustaceans.

## DATA FILE

 **PREDATOR POWER**

 **SIZE**: Up to 1.4 m (4.6 ft) long

 **DISTRIBUTION**: Coastal waters of north-eastern Atlantic Ocean and Mediterranean Sea

 **DIET**: Crustaceans

Grey or brownish body lacks darker markings

Tiny, star-like spots

This shark uses its small, **grinding teeth** to **crunch** the **shells of crabs**.

# GUMMY SHARK
*Mustelus antarcticus*

Sometimes a predator needs jaws for crunching, rather than for slicing. This species of hound shark has flat teeth for cracking the hard shells of crustaceans. It swims near the bottom around the cooler parts of Australia, where females give birth in shallow nurseries.

Jaws are packed with flat teeth for crushing hard-shelled prey

# BANDED HOUND SHARK
*Triakis scyllium*

Like most members of the hound shark family, this species has a restricted range of distribution – in coastal waters around Japan and eastern Asia. This suggests this shark rarely travels long distances. It is especially common in muddy estuaries and bays, where it lives among seaweeds and eelgrass.

Small, dark spots and blotches

Inshore marauders

146

Small, white spots on a
bronze- or grey-coloured body

## DATA FILE

**PREDATOR POWER**

**SIZE:** Up to 1.8 m (5.9 ft) long

**DISTRIBUTION:** Waters off
southern Australia and Tasmania

**DIET:** Crustaceans, worms, and fish

The gummy
shark has a
maximum
**lifespan of
16 years**.

Short, rounded snout

## DATA FILE

**PREDATOR POWER**

**SIZE:** Up to 1.5 m (4.9 ft) long

**DISTRIBUTION:** Coastal waters of
Japan and eastern Asia

**DIET:** Small fish, crustaceans, and
other invertebrates

The banded
hound shark
gives birth to
**up to 24 pups
per litter**.

Inshore marauders

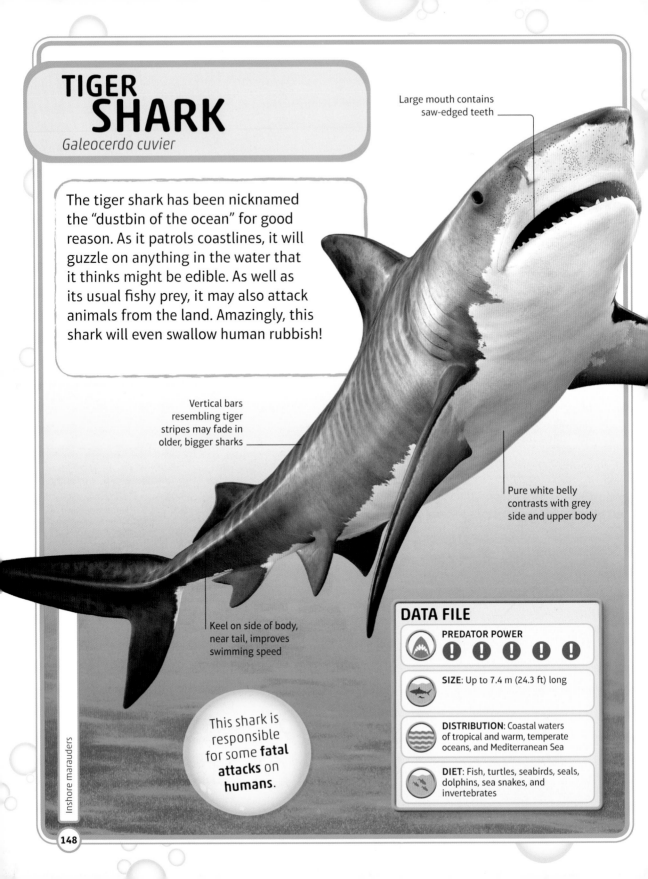

# TIGER
# SHARK

*Galeocerdo cuvier*

The tiger shark has been nicknamed the "dustbin of the ocean" for good reason. As it patrols coastlines, it will guzzle on anything in the water that it thinks might be edible. As well as its usual fishy prey, it may also attack animals from the land. Amazingly, this shark will even swallow human rubbish!

Large mouth contains saw-edged teeth

Vertical bars resembling tiger stripes may fade in older, bigger sharks

Pure white belly contrasts with grey side and upper body

Keel on side of body, near tail, improves swimming speed

This shark is responsible for some **fatal attacks** on **humans**.

## DATA FILE

**PREDATOR POWER**

**SIZE**: Up to 7.4 m (24.3 ft) long

**DISTRIBUTION**: Coastal waters of tropical and warm, temperate oceans, and Mediterranean Sea

**DIET**: Fish, turtles, seabirds, seals, dolphins, sea snakes, and invertebrates

Inshore marauders

# LEMON SHARK
## *Negaprion brevirostris*

Warm, sunny lagoons are the favourite habitat of this tropical hunter. After mating, pregnant female lemon sharks gather in the lagoons of the Caribbean to give birth. Baby lemon sharks will spend their early years here, growing up in the safety of a tropical nursery.

## DATA FILE

 **PREDATOR POWER**

 **SIZE**: Up to 3.4 m (11.2 ft) long

 **HABITAT**: Warm, shallow coastal waters of tropical Atlantic and Pacific oceans

 **DIET**: Fish and, sometimes, seabirds

Up to **500 baby lemon sharks** can live in a single nursery.

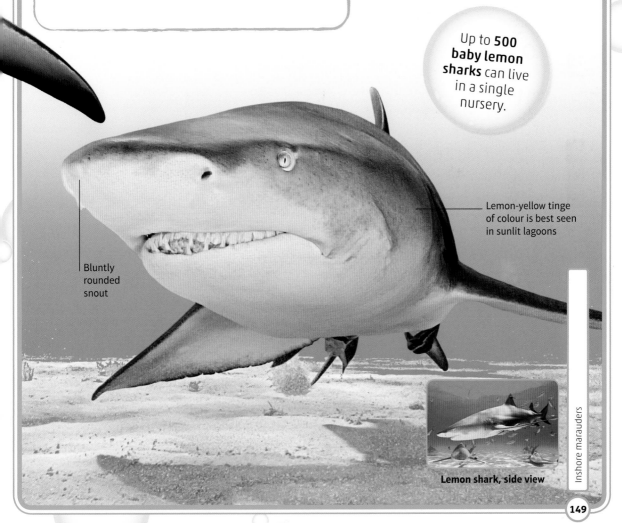

Lemon-yellow tinge of colour is best seen in sunlit lagoons

Bluntly rounded snout

**Lemon shark, side view**

Inshore marauders

# BULL
# SHARK
*Carcharhinus leucas*

Big, triangular, first dorsal fin may stick out of the water when the shark is in the shallows _____

The bull shark lives in coastal waters that are often made murky by mud running in from the land, but it regularly goes beyond the estuaries to swim up rivers. Adventurous bull sharks can travel thousands of kilometres inland, sometimes crossing rapids to do so.

## DATA FILE

 **PREDATOR POWER**
! ! ! ! !

 **SIZE**: Up to 3.4 m (11 ft) long

 **DISTRIBUTION**: Coastal waters and rivers, and in tropical and warm, temperate oceans

 **DIET**: Fish, crustaceans, turtles, echinoderms, birds, and mammals

150

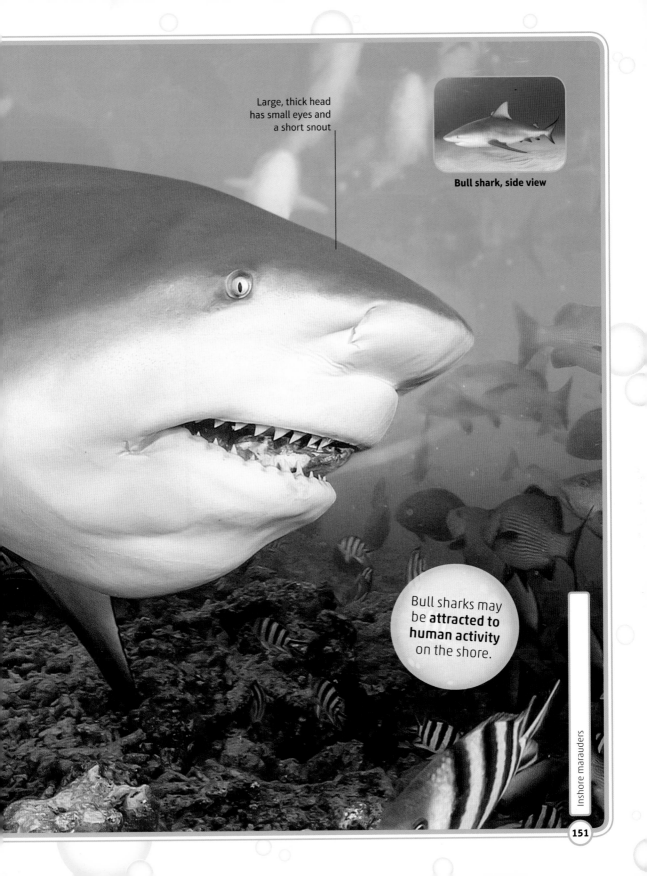

Large, thick head has small eyes and a short snout

**Bull shark, side view**

Bull sharks may be **attracted to human activity** on the shore.

# SARCASTIC FRINGEHEAD

*Neoclinus blanchardi*

The extraordinary threat display of this fish is worse than its bite. The fringehead spends much of its time in a burrow, occasionally coming out to hunt shrimps and small crabs. If two fringeheads come face to face, they flare out their jaws to show that each is the boss of its own territory.

## DATA FILE

 **PREDATOR POWER**
❗ ❗ ⬤ ⬤ ⬤

 **SIZE**: Up to 30 cm (11.8 in) long

 **DISTRIBUTION**: Coastal waters off California

**DIET**: Crustaceans

Much of the eel-like body is concealed inside a burrow or tube

 Inshore marauders

**Fringehead, top view**

# ATLANTIC
# WOLF-FISH
*Anarhichas lupus*

The formidable jaws and teeth of the wolf-fish are good for eating snails, crabs, and sea urchins. Crunching through hard shells is no problem for this cold-water predator. Unlike most oceanic bony fish – which scatter their eggs in the water for fertilization – this fish has internal fertilization. The males protect the brood in a nest for several months.

## DATA FILE

 **PREDATOR POWER**

 **SIZE**: Up to 1.5 m (4.9 ft) long

 **DISTRIBUTION**: Cold coastal waters of North Atlantic Ocean

 **DIET**: Molluscs, crustaceans, and echinoderms

Dagger-like teeth at the front are so big they protrude from the mouth

A substance in this fish's blood keeps it **flowing in the cold**.

Atlantic wolf-fish, side view

Inshore marauders

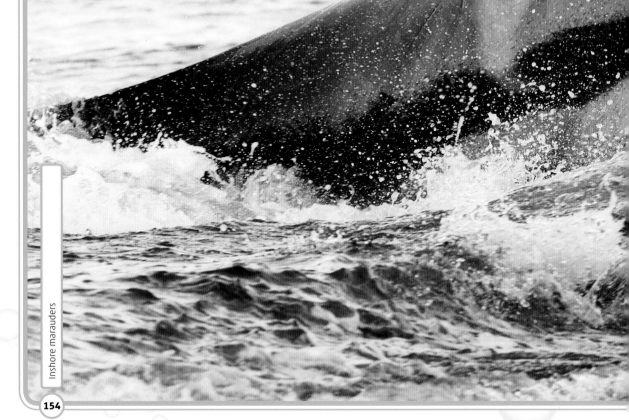

# KILLER WHALE
*Orcinus orca*

The killer whale, also called orca, is the biggest member of the dolphin family. Like other dolphins, it has a taste for fish. However, it hunts big marine mammals too, and regularly comes close to the shoreline on the trail of seals. Killer whales travel together in groups called "pods", which sometimes consist of more than 50 individuals.

Dorsal fin in adult is the biggest of any marine mammal, and is as tall as an adult human. The dorsal fin of males is much bigger than that of females (female in image).

**Killer whale, side view**

Black upper side contrasts sharply with white underside and patches behind eyes

## DATA FILE

**PREDATOR POWER**
! ! ! ! !

**SIZE**: Up to 9.5 m (31.2 ft) long

**DISTRIBUTION**: Coastal waters worldwide, but mainly in cooler regions

**DIET**: Fish, squid, seals, dolphins, and marine birds

Killer whales **hunt in teams** to catch seals.

# LEOPARD SEAL
*Hydrurga leptonyx*

Stocky head with strong jaws

Most kinds of seals hunt fish only, but the leopard seal sometimes likes meatier prey. Although its teeth are not as dagger-like as those of many land carnivores, its jaws are very strong, and it is capable of killing a penguin by shaking it. This seal waits to grab a penguin as it jumps into the water, and sometimes smacks it on the water's surface to knock it senseless.

Scattered, dark spots give the leopard seal its name

The leopard seal **interlocks its teeth** to strain krill from the water.

**Leopard seal, side view**

## DATA FILE

 **PREDATOR POWER**

 **SIZE**: Up to 3.4 m (11.2 ft) long

 **DISTRIBUTION**: Rocky coastlines and coastal waters around Antarctica

 **DIET**: Fish, squid and octopuses, krill, other seals, and penguins

# SOUTHERN ELEPHANT SEAL

*Mirounga leonina*

This seal is the **heaviest land-going marine carnivore**.

An elephant seal can spend up to eight months of the year out at sea fishing for food. This giant among seals can dive more than 1 km (0.6 miles) below the surface for fish, and can hold its breath for up to two hours – longer than most other marine mammals. However, when it is time to breed, the southern elephant seal returns to shore to mate and give birth, like other seals.

## DATA FILE

**PREDATOR POWER**

 **SIZE**: 3–5 m (9.8–16.4 ft) long; males are bigger, and much heavier, than females

 **DISTRIBUTION**: Coastlines and coastal ocean waters of Antarctica and southern tip of South America

 **DIET**: Fish and squid

Males use their fleshy proboscis (long nose) to louden their roar

**Southern elephant seal, side view**

# SEA OTTER

*Enhydris lutris*

## DATA FILE

**PREDATOR POWER**

**SIZE:** Up to 1.5 m (4.9 ft) long

**HABITAT:** North Pacific shorelines and coastal waters of Russia and North America

**DIET:** Molluscs, crabs, and sea urchins

The sea otter is the smallest marine mammal. It lacks the thick blubber of bigger ocean mammals, so stays warm in cold Pacific waters with a fur coat so dense that little of the animal's precious body heat escapes. Sea otters pick up rocks with their front paws and use them to smash open clams and other prey. They can even do this on the flat of their bellies while floating on their back in the water.

Sea otter, front view

Dense fur keeps otter warm, so it can float on its back in icy water

Sea otters have the **densest fur of any mammal**.

# EMPEROR PENGUIN
*Aptenodytes forsteri*

Small feathers trap air close to the body to help with insulation

This is the only animal that **breeds on mainland Antarctica** during winter.

Wings flap up and down for propulsion

Emperor penguin, side view

Emperor penguins hunt fish in the icy waters around Antarctica, but, remarkably, also journey into the frozen continent on foot to breed. Here the males endure the bitter polar winter as they incubate their eggs, waiting for the females to bring a meal of fish once the eggs have hatched.

## DATA FILE

**PREDATOR POWER** ❗ ❗ ● ● ●

**SIZE**: Up to 1.2 m (3.9 ft) high

**HABITAT**: Shorelines and coastal waters of Antarctica

**DIET**: Fish, squid, and krill

Inshore marauders

# SALTWATER
# CROCODILE
*Crocodylus porosus*

The world's largest reptile, the saltwater crocodile is a predator of tropical swamplands. It can snatch large mammals from the waterside, pulling them into the water, while rolling over to drown its prey. Unlike other crocodilians, it tolerates saltwater, so regularly swims out to sea, sometimes reaching remote oceanic islands.

Saltwater crocodiles can stay submerged in water for **up to 2 hours**.

Darker markings on yellowish scales fade as animal grows older

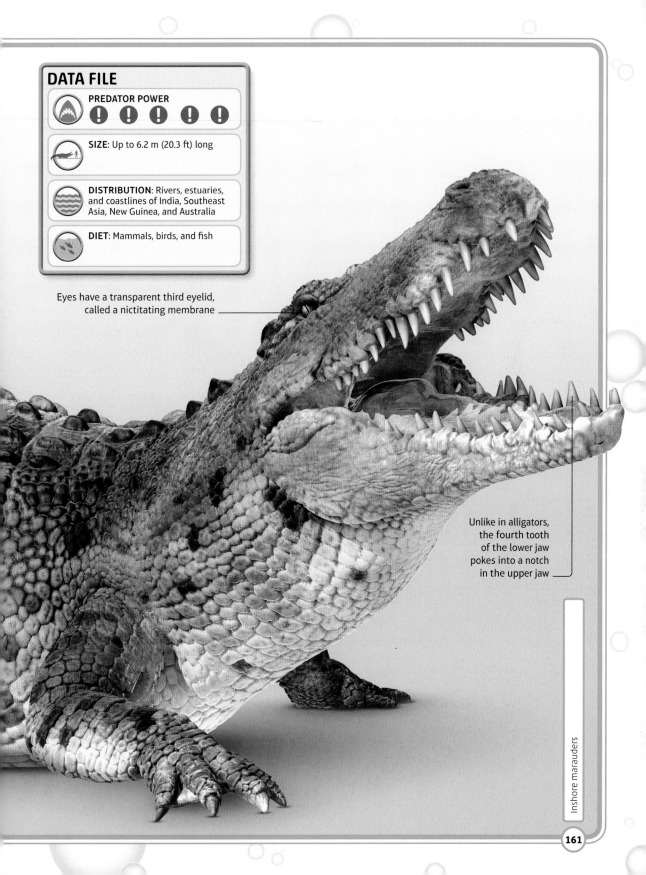

## DATA FILE

**PREDATOR POWER**
❗ ❗ ❗ ❗ ❗

**SIZE:** Up to 6.2 m (20.3 ft) long

**DISTRIBUTION:** Rivers, estuaries, and coastlines of India, Southeast Asia, New Guinea, and Australia

**DIET:** Mammals, birds, and fish

Eyes have a transparent third eyelid, called a nictitating membrane

Unlike in alligators, the fourth tooth of the lower jaw pokes into a notch in the upper jaw

# SEA SNAKE

*Hydrophis sp.*

Probably no other reptile is as well adapted to ocean life as a sea snake. Unlike turtles, which have to lay eggs on land, sea snakes give birth to live young in the water. These snakes are close relatives of land cobras and share their potent venom, using it to immobilize their prey.

Sea snakes have **one of the strongest venoms** of any snake.

Paddle-like tail propels snake in water

No enlarged belly scales for gripping ground, such as in land-living snakes

Inshore marauders

162

# NAUTILUS
*Nautilus pompilius*

The nautilus is often described as a "living fossil", because it has changed very little over millions of years of evolution. It belongs to a group of animals called cephalopods, which includes the squid and octopus. Its tentacles are too feeble to tackle big prey, and its jet-propelled swimming movements are rather sluggish.

**Jet propulsion** helps it move backwards in water.

Whorled, chambered shell

Has more tentacles than either a squid or an octopus

Inshore marauders

# PEACOCK
# MANTIS SHRIMP
*Odontodactylus scyllarus*

Highly sophisticated eyes provide the most complex colour vision of any animal

A mantis shrimp can **smash its way out** of an aquarium.

Claws modified into clubs

There are two kinds of mantis shrimp – stabbers and smashers. Stabbers have spiny claws that spear prey, but the colourful peacock mantis shrimp uses a club to smash through shells. The mantis shrimp lives in a burrow, the entrance of which is usually littered with the broken fragments of its prey.

## DATA FILE

**PREDATOR POWER**

**SIZE:** Up to 18 cm (7.1 in) long

**DISTRIBUTION:** Tropical coastal waters of Indian and western Pacific oceans

**DIET:** Shelled molluscs and crustaceans

Inshore marauders

# SMOOTH-CLAWED
# PISTOL SHRIMP

*Alpheus paracrinitus*

The snapping pincers make **much of the underwater noise** in the ocean.

This little shrimp disables prey in a remarkable way. It has a special claw that can snap shut with such speed and force that it generates shock waves. These are powerful enough to stun small animals nearby. The shrimp then drags the immobile victims into its lair to eat them alive.

Bold, coloured patterns

Enlarged pincer generates shock waves

## DATA FILE

 **PREDATOR POWER**
❗ ❗

 **SIZE**: Up to 1.8 cm (0.7 in) long

 **DISTRIBUTION**: Tropical reefs of Atlantic Ocean and Caribbean Sea

 **DIET**: Other small crustaceans and small fish

Inshore marauders

# 8

# PREDATORS OF THE REEF

Tropical coral reefs are extremely rich in ocean life. Coral not only forms an ocean habitat, but is itself a predator. In warm, sunny waters, it grows into huge rocky colonies, which are covered in billions of plankton-grabbing tentacles. Many predators live on the reef, including many species of shark.

# BLACKTIP
# SHARK
*Carcharhinus limbatus*

Fin tips are often black, but the markings may fade in older sharks

The blacktip shark thrives in shallow waters around estuaries and muddy mangrove swamps. It is an acrobatic predator that gathers in large numbers to charge at shoaling fish. When doing this, blacktip sharks will sometimes jump right out of the water and spin around in midair.

The blacktip shark can **spin three times** when it jumps out of the water.

## DATA FILE

 **PREDATOR POWER**

 **SIZE**: Up to 2.6 m (8.5 ft) long

 **DISTRIBUTION**: Coral reefs of warm, temperate and tropical oceans, and Mediterranean and Red seas

 **DIET**: Fish, crustaceans, and squid

# OCEANIC WHITETIP SHARK
*Carcharhinus longimanus*

One of the most abundant of all sharks, the oceanic whitetip shark is especially common around remote islands, but can also wander far from the shore. It is not as speedy as some other open-ocean sharks, but it is more aggressive around prey, especially when it gathers together in groups.

Long, paddle-like pectoral fins spread wide as the shark cruises beneath the ocean surface

The whitetip shark **bullies smaller sharks** at feeding frenzies.

## DATA FILE

**PREDATOR POWER**

**SIZE**: Up to 3.9 m (12.8 ft) long

**DISTRIBUTION**: Surface waters of open oceans and island coastlines in tropical and subtropical regions

**DIET**: Large fish, squid, seabirds, and mammals

# SILKY
# SHARK
*Carcharhinus falciformis*

## DATA FILE

 **PREDATOR POWER**

 **SIZE:** Up to 3.3 m (10.8 ft) long

 **DISTRIBUTION:** Coastal and open waters of tropical oceans and Mediterranean Sea

 **DIET:** Fish, squid, and swimming crabs

Most of the silky sharks seen swimming over reefs close to the shore are likely to be immature ones. As individuals of this species grow older, they spend more time in the open ocean. The silky shark has especially sensitive hearing, which helps it home in on the deep, rumbling sounds coming from a shark feeding frenzy.

The silky shark's **smooth skin** gives this hunter its name.

Smooth skin is due to network of tiny, densely-packed denticles (tiny, tooth-like scales)

Upper body may appear blackish

Long, narrow pectoral fin

# DUSKY SHARK
*Carcharhinus obscurus*

The dusky shark can often be seen **tailing ships**.

Grey- or bronze-coloured upper body

Dusky-tipped fin is not as boldly marked as in some other related species

Like many of the related reef sharks, the dusky shark likes warm waters, although it migrates away from the tropics during the hottest months of the year. Females move closer to shore to give birth to their pups. Here, the youngsters will gather in shoals before they grow into adults and venture out into deeper water.

## DATA FILE

 **PREDATOR POWER**

**SIZE:** Up to 4 m (13.1 ft) long

**DISTRIBUTION:** Coastal waters in tropical and warm, temperate oceans worldwide

**DIET:** Fish (including other sharks) and crustaceans

Predators of the reef

# GALAPAGOS
# SHARK
*Carcharhinus galapagensis*

This shark may **hunch its back** to threaten nearby divers.

Grey-brown upper body fades to whitish below

Large, sickle-shaped pectoral fins may have dusky tips

Despite its name, the Galapagos shark is not confined to the Pacific Ocean's Galapagos Islands, but lives around most tropical islands on Earth. It apparently favours rocky habitats, in which the currents can be especially strong. This shark swims in groups and has a reputation for being aggressive, even dominating other kinds of shark near prey.

## DATA FILE

 **PREDATOR POWER**

 **SIZE**: Possibly up to 3.7 m (12.1 ft) long

 **DISTRIBUTION**: Coastal waters around islands in warm, temperate and tropical oceans worldwide

 **DIET**: Mainly bottom-living fish

# CARIBBEAN
# REEF SHARK
*Carcharhinus perezi*

The Caribbean reef shark lies motionless, seemingly asleep, in caves or on the ocean floor. This allows divers to approach it, making it quite popular with tourist divers. This tropical American predator uses the muscles at the back of its throat to pump water over its gills, supplying them with oxygen.

Upper body is dark greyish or brownish in colour

Faint, white band on the side of the body near the rear, like in related sharks

Large, narrow pectoral fins

## DATA FILE

 **PREDATOR POWER**

 **SIZE:** Up to 3 m (9.8 ft) long

 **DISTRIBUTION:** Coastal waters and river mouths of western Atlantic Ocean and Caribbean Sea

 **DIET:** Fish

This docile shark only **rarely tries to bite** human divers.

# BLACKTIP
# REEF SHARK
*Carcharhinus melanopterus*

One of the most common species of reef shark in the tropical Indo-Pacific, the blacktip reef shark is a fast-moving predator. It stays in midwater or close to the bottom, but sometimes moves into the shallows, where its dorsal fin can be seen sticking up out of the water. It even occasionally ventures into brackish (slightly salty) waters of estuaries.

Prominent black fin tips are underlined with white

White band runs along side of body towards the rear

Short, rounded snout

## DATA FILE

 **PREDATOR POWER**

**SIZE**: Up to 2 m (6.6 ft) long

**DISTRIBUTION**: Coral reefs of tropical Indian and western Pacific oceans, and Mediterranean and Red seas

**DIET**: Fish, crustaceans, squid, and molluscs

This shark will not leave its **favourite patch** of reef for **years on end**.

Predators of the reef

# GREY REEF SHARK

*Carcharhinus amblyrhynchos*

Very popular with tourists, the grey reef shark is a highly common reef shark in the tropics. It swims in groups in shallow water and is sometimes curious enough to approach divers. At night, the groups seem to get more restless and disperse into more open waters.

White underside contrasts with grey upper body

Pregnant female **grey reef sharks** may gather in **large groups**.

Black-tipped fins

## DATA FILE

 **PREDATOR POWER**

 **SIZE:** Possibly up to 2.5 m (8.2 ft) long

 **DISTRIBUTION:** Coastal waters of tropical and warm, temperate Indian and western Pacific oceans

 **DIET:** Fish, squid, octopuses, and crustaceans

Predators of the reef

# BRONZE WHALER

*Carcharhinus brachyurus*

Greyish upper body has a bronze sheen

The bronze whaler **grows slower** than most other kinds of shark.

Long pectoral fins

Black fin edges may be clearer on some fins than others

Each year large numbers of the bronze whaler gather along the East African coast to follow the sardine run, a seasonal northwards migration of massive shoals of sardines that attracts many of the ocean's predators. Bronze whalers in other parts of the world also make small migrations, but the reasons are not always clear.

## DATA FILE

**PREDATOR POWER**

**SIZE**: Up to 2.9 m (9.5 ft) long

**DISTRIBUTION**: Coastal waters of Atlantic, Pacific, and Indian oceans, and Mediterranean Sea

**DIET**: Fish, squid, and octopuses

# BLUE SHARK

*Prionace glauca*

Unlike the related reef sharks, the blue shark spends much of its life away from coastlines. By hunting in groups, it can make shoals of prey bunch together, even in the wide expanse of the open ocean. These hunters take turns to grab a mouthful from the gathered prey.

Often hunting in packs, blue sharks are called the **"wolves of the sea"**.

Long, narrow pectoral fins are good for turning at speed while swimming

These sharks feed predominantly at night and probably use their large, well-developed eyes at close range to detect bioluminescence

## DATA FILE

 **PREDATOR POWER**

 **SIZE**: Up to 3.8 m (12.5 ft) long

 **DISTRIBUTION**: Open ocean worldwide, except in the coldest regions, and Mediterranean Sea

 **DIET**: Fish, squid, other invertebrates, and seabirds

Predators of the reef

# WHITETIP
# REEF SHARK

*Triaenodon obesus*

The whitetip reef shark prowls the rocky crevices of a tropical reef in search of prey. Small fish dart between rocks that provide a safe hiding spot, but this shark's small, slender body is perfect for reaching them. Sometimes, if the shark fails to make a grab straight away, it waits patiently between the rocks until its prey emerges.

Slender body and extra tough skin help the shark hunt easily among rocks

Strong brow ridges protect the eyes of the shark as it probes between rocks for prey

## DATA FILE

 **PREDATOR POWER**

 **SIZE**: Up to 1.6 m (5.2 ft) long

 **DISTRIBUTION**: Coral reefs of tropical Indian and Pacific oceans, and Red Sea

 **DIET**: Fish, octopuses, lobsters, and crabs

Predators of the reef

178

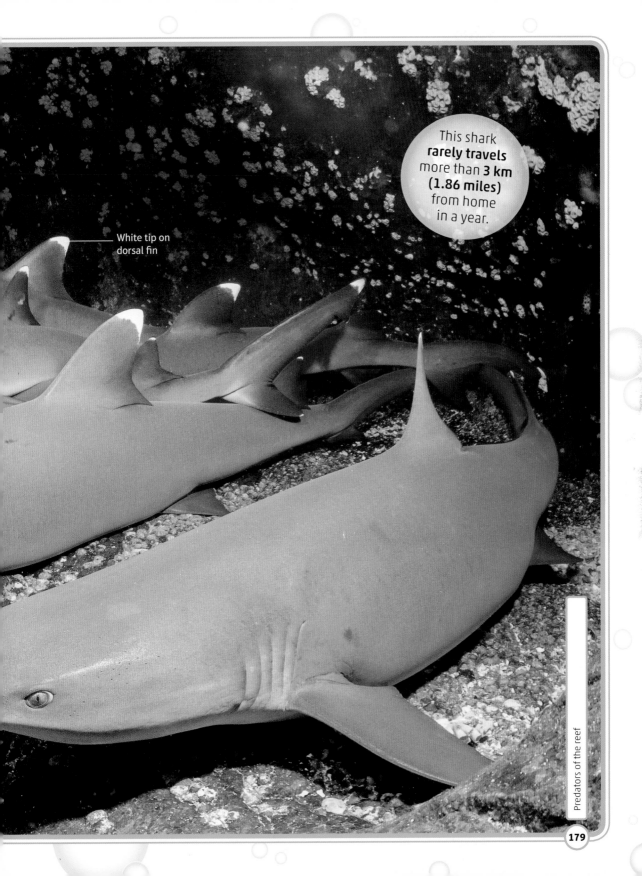

White tip on dorsal fin

This shark **rarely travels** more than **3 km (1.86 miles)** from home in a year.

# GREAT HAMMERHEAD

*Sphyrna mokarran*

The great hammerhead shark may swim over coral reefs, but it often goes further into the open ocean on its journey to new coastlines. Like other hammerheads, the great hammerhead sweeps the ocean bottom with its "hammer" to sense bottom-living prey and has a particular taste for stingrays.

Enormous, first dorsal fin stands higher than those of any other hammerhead

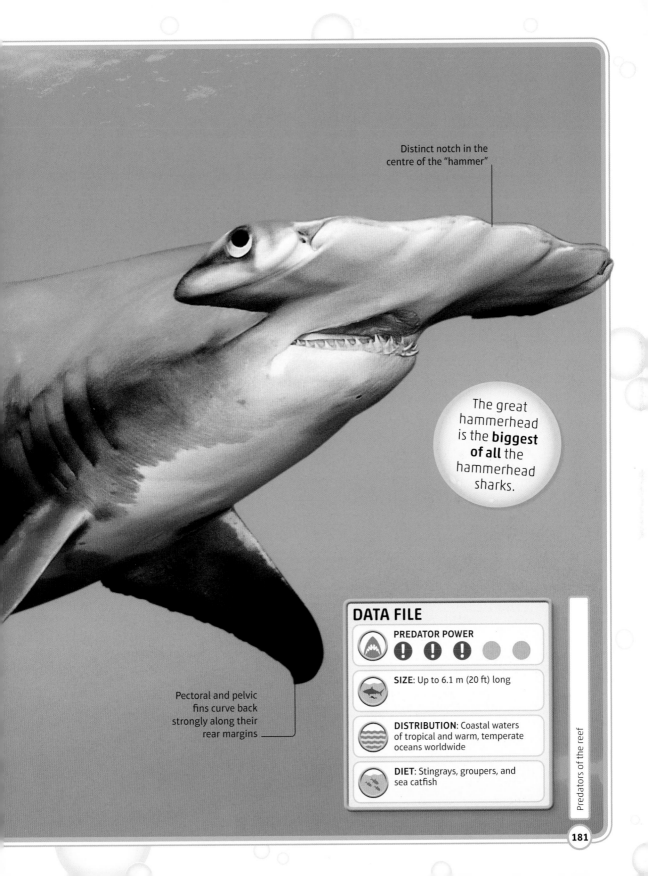

Distinct notch in the centre of the "hammer"

The great hammerhead is the **biggest of all** the hammerhead sharks.

Pectoral and pelvic fins curve back strongly along their rear margins

## DATA FILE

**PREDATOR POWER**

**SIZE:** Up to 6.1 m (20 ft) long

**DISTRIBUTION:** Coastal waters of tropical and warm, temperate oceans worldwide

**DIET:** Stingrays, groupers, and sea catfish

# SCALLOPED HAMMERHEAD

*Sphyrna lewini*

Eyes on hammer tips give a wide field of view

Front edge of hammer is wavy

The hammerhead shark's wide head is packed with sensors that detect the movement and scent of prey. The scalloped hammerhead has a taste for stingrays buried in mud and sand. To find its prey, it sweeps its head over the ocean bottom, like a metal detector, grabbing any ray hidden beneath.

The hammer **provides the hammerhead with lift** when swimming.

## DATA FILE

**PREDATOR POWER**

**SIZE:** Up to 4.2 m (13.8 ft) long

**DISTRIBUTION:** Coastal ocean waters worldwide

**DIET:** Fish (including other sharks and rays) and invertebrates

# CROWN-OF-THORNS
# STARFISH
*Acanthaster planci*

Here is the ultimate enemy of coral. It is one of the biggest of all starfish and has an appetite to match. It creeps on tiny tube feet over the surface of a coral colony, nibbling away at the fleshy polyps. Few animals can eat this starfish, and so heavy infestations of the crown-of-thorns can cause serious damage to a reef.

Spines can transfer poison, causing swelling and pain to human skin

Up to 21 arms

A single starfish **can kill 6 sq m (64.6 sq ft)** of coral in a year.

# GREEN MORAY EEL

*Gymnothorax funebris*

Morays include the biggest kinds of eel. Most live in rocky lairs on coral reefs and rely on surprise to ambush passing prey. Some morays seem to cooperate with predatory grouper fish in driving prey into the open from between rocks – so both hunters end up with a share of the meal.

Mouth is kept open to keep water moving through small gill openings

Morays have an **extra set of jaws** in their throat that pop out to grab prey.

Yellowish or greenish colour comes from a protective mucus coating

## DATA FILE

### PREDATOR POWER

**SIZE:** Up to 2.5 m (8.2 ft) long

**DISTRIBUTION:** Tropical coastal waters of the Gulf of Mexico and Caribbean Sea

**DIET:** Fish, crabs, squid, and shrimps

# HUMPHEAD WRASSE
*Cheilinus undulatus*

This reef-dwelling fish is a big, unfussy predator and will tackle prey that many other hunters find distasteful or even poisonous. Juveniles usually stay hidden among rocks and seaweed, but big adults patrol more open water on the edge of the reef. Adults change sex when they reach maturity, turning from female to male after about nine years.

This fish may **eat poisonous animals**, such as crown-of-thorns starfish.

Forehead hump is prominent in bigger, older individuals

Thick, fleshy lips

# BRAIN CORAL
*Colpophyllia natans*

Coral may look like lifeless rock, but in fact it is a colony of tiny predators. At night, its rocky skeleton comes alive with thousands of tiny polyps. Each polyp is like a miniature anemone, with a ring of little tentacles for catching plankton, and a central mouth for swallowing the tiny meal.

Coral colonies **release eggs and sperms simultaneously**.

Ridges of the skeleton make the colony's surface look like a human brain

# MAGNIFICENT
# SEA ANEMONE
*Heteractis magnifica*

Anemones may look like plants, but they are actually predatory animals. Their muscular tentacles are armed with microscopic stingers that paralyse small prey. The magnificent sea anemone supplements this diet by making use of algae that live in its flesh. These use light energy in bright sunlight to provide sugar through a process called photosynthesis.

Clown fish families often live in the **tentacles of sea anemones**.

Stinging tentacles catch plankton and transfer it to the mouth in the centre _____

## DATA FILE

 **PREDATOR POWER**

 **SIZE**: Up to 50 cm (19.7 in) in diameter

 **DISTRIBUTION**: Coral reefs of tropical Indian and western Pacific oceans, and Red Sea

 **DIET**: Small invertebrates and tiny fish; some food is made by algae living in the anemone's flesh

Column contains the stomach for digesting prey

# HARLEQUIN SHRIMP

*Hymenocera picta*

## DATA FILE

 **PREDATOR POWER**

 **SIZE**: Up to 5 cm (2 in) long

 **DISTRIBUTION**: Tropical coastal waters of Indian and western Pacific oceans

**DIET**: Starfish and sometimes sea urchins

This colourful, little shrimp has a taste for starfish flesh and little else, and will go to extraordinary lengths to get a meal. The harlequin shrimp is strong and nimble enough to carry a small starfish back to its burrow. Once there, it uses the starfish as a kind of living larder, feeding on it one leg at a time.

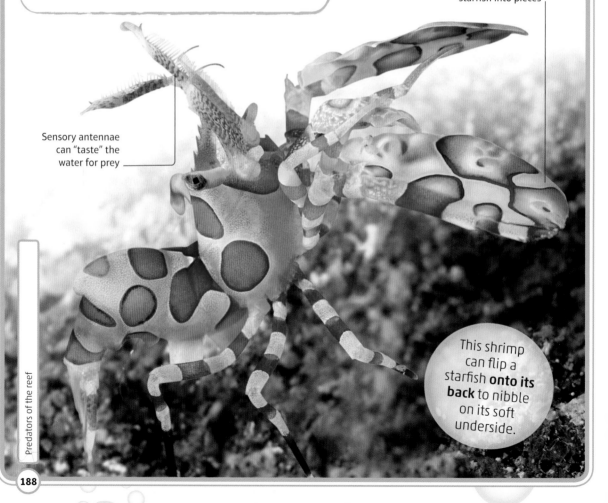

Sharp claws help tear starfish into pieces

Sensory antennae can "taste" the water for prey

This shrimp can flip a starfish **onto its back** to nibble on its soft underside.

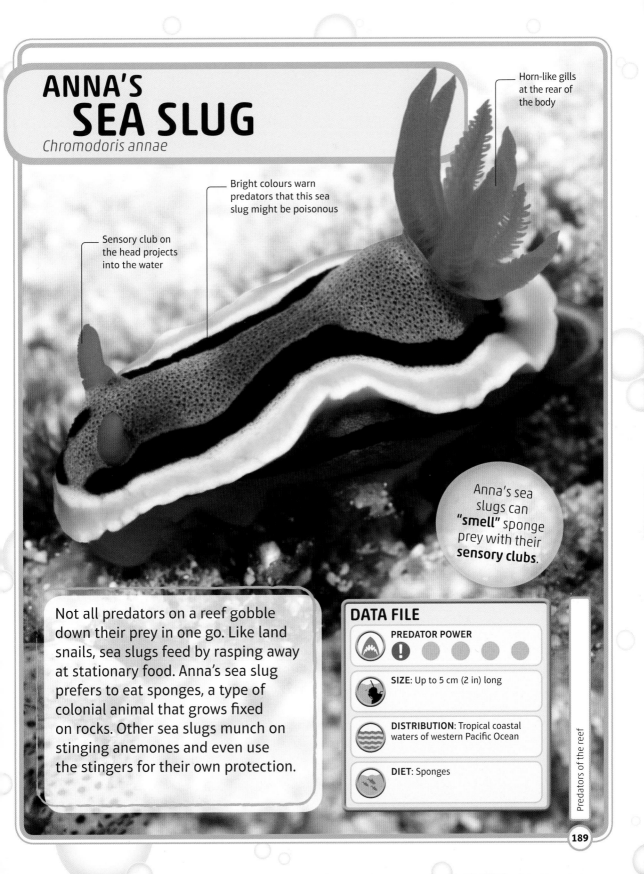

# ANNA'S SEA SLUG
*Chromodoris annae*

Horn-like gills at the rear of the body

Bright colours warn predators that this sea slug might be poisonous

Sensory club on the head projects into the water

Anna's sea slugs can **"smell"** sponge prey with their **sensory clubs**.

Not all predators on a reef gobble down their prey in one go. Like land snails, sea slugs feed by rasping away at stationary food. Anna's sea slug prefers to eat sponges, a type of colonial animal that grows fixed on rocks. Other sea slugs munch on stinging anemones and even use the stingers for their own protection.

## DATA FILE

**PREDATOR POWER**

**SIZE:** Up to 5 cm (2 in) long

**DISTRIBUTION:** Tropical coastal waters of western Pacific Ocean

**DIET:** Sponges

Predators of the reef

# REFERENCE

Sharks include some of the most formidable predators of the ocean. Practically every ocean habitat, from the intertidal shallows to the deepest abyss, is home to sharks. Their family tree extends back hundreds of millions of years, but these are no primitive survivors of a bygone age – modern sharks have sharp senses for finding prey and sophisticated ways of raising their young.

# THE SHARK FAMILY TREE

Sharks have been hunting the oceans since before the time of the dinosaurs. Together with chimaeras and rays, they belong to a group of fish with a skeleton made from mineralized cartilage, rather than bone. About 500 shark species in nine main groups are around today, but many other shark-like fish that lived millions of years ago are now extinct.

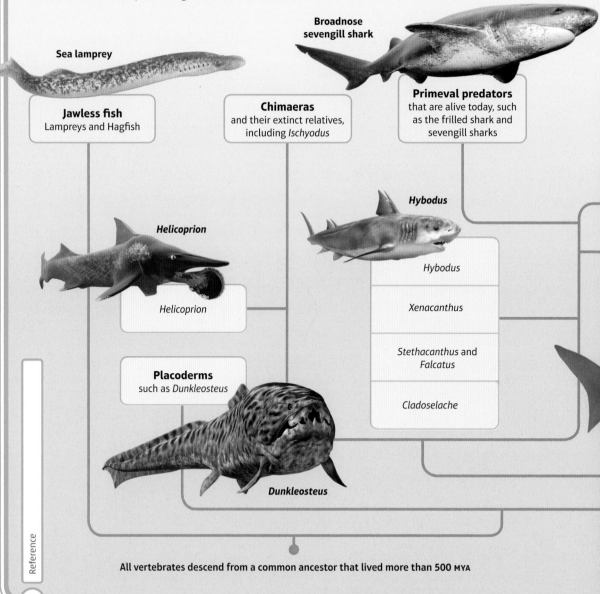

**Broadnose sevengill shark**

**Sea lamprey**

**Jawless fish**
Lampreys and Hagfish

**Chimaeras**
and their extinct relatives, including *Ischyodus*

**Primeval predators**
that are alive today, such as the frilled shark and sevengill sharks

*Helicoprion*

*Hybodus*

*Helicoprion*

| Hybodus |
| *Xenacanthus* |
| *Stethacanthus* and *Falcatus* |
| *Cladoselache* |

**Placoderms**
such as *Dunkleosteus*

*Dunkleosteus*

**All vertebrates descend from a common ancestor that lived more than 500 MYA**

**Horn shark,
an example of a
bullhead shark**

**Killers between
the tides** such as
wobbegongs and
bullhead sharks

**Open-ocean
cruisers and chasers**
such as the
great white shark

**Mud-rooting
monsters**
such as sawsharks and
angelsharks

**Muscle-mouthed
gulpers** such as the
whale shark and
the nurse shark

**Devils of the dark**
such as lantern sharks,
spiny dogfish, and
sleeper sharks

**Inshore marauders**
such as cat sharks
and reef sharks

## THE EVIDENCE

Scientists use different methods to
work out how groups of animals
have evolved. They look for
similarities in living sharks and their
DNA, and study fossils of prehistoric
species. But cartilaginous skeletons
of sharks do not preserve well, and
fossilized teeth sometimes provide
the only evidence from the past.

18 cm (7 in)

**Fossilized
*Megalodon* tooth**

**Rays**

**Modern bony
fish and
other vertebrates**

*Leedsichthys*

*Leedsichthys*

***Acanthodes*, a
Carboniferous
spiny "shark"**

*Acanthodes*

**KEY**

Living        Extinct

# THE SHARK MACHINE

Most sharks are big, torpedo-shaped predators that swim through open water, but some have a flattened body for settling on the sea floor. A few others filter plankton from water instead of biting prey. Like most other fish, sharks have paired pectoral and pelvic fins for steering, and dorsal and anal fins for stabilizing the body's posture in the water. Power for movement comes from the shark's beating tail.

**Skeleton**
The spine and rest of the shark's skeleton is made from cartilage that is hardened by minerals. The skeleton of most other vertebrates is mainly made of bone, which is even harder.

Second dorsal fin is absent in some sharks

**Tail**
The spine runs upwards into the top section (lobe) of the tail, which is usually bigger than the lower section.

Anal fin

Pelvic fin (one of a pair)

**Skin**
Shark skin feels rough like sandpaper, because it is covered with tiny, tooth-like prickles called "dermal denticles".

**Oily liver**
Unlike most bony fishes, sharks do not have a gas-filled swim bladder to stay buoyant. Instead, buoyancy comes from an extra-oily liver.

Reference

First dorsal fin is usually bigger than second

### Gill arches

This cage-like part of the skeleton supports the shark's gills, which extract oxygen from water. The water enters through the mouth, moves over the gills, and then runs out from the slits, of which most sharks have five.

### Super senses

The skin has jelly-filled pores (ampullae of Lorenzini), which are especially packed on the snout. These pores are sensitive to the electrical activity given off by the muscles and nerves of prey.

Upper jaw is loosely connected to the skull, enabling it to extend easily

Lower jaw can also be extended

Pectoral fin (one of a pair)

## JAWS AND TEETH

Sharks are predators – some filter feed, while others use their jaws to bite into their prey. Some sharks can protrude their jaws further than others.

**Cutting teeth of great white shark**

**Grinding teeth of bullhead shark**

**Projectile jaws of goblin shark**

**Gouging jaws of cookiecutter shark**

# SHARKS AS HUNTERS

All sharks get their food by eating other animals. A few, such as the whale shark, are filter-feeders, who strain tiny animals from the ocean's floating plankton. Other sharks scavenge on dead material and will even follow fishing boats to grab leftovers. However, most kinds of shark hunt, bite, and kill living prey. They have an impressive array of sense organs for hunting. The smallest sharks target fish and invertebrates, but some of the biggest hunters prey on animals up to the size of dolphins and seals.

## MORE THAN 1 KM (¹/₂ MILE) AWAY

## LESS THAN 1 KM (¹/₂ MILE) AWAY

**Smelling the blood**
Sharks can detect the presence of prey across kilometres of ocean water by using the super-sensitive smell and taste receptors in their nostrils and mouth. Some sharks are said to be able to sniff a drop of blood 5 km (3.1 miles) away.

**Listening for movement**
Sharks can hear the sound of an animal splashing about in the water, and some are good at homing in on the thrashing noises made by a so-called "feeding frenzy", in which lots of sharks gather to feast on meat.

**Feeling the movement**
A series of pores run in a so-called lateral line down the side of the shark's body. Seawater seeping into these pores goes through tiny tubes containing sensors that detect changing water currents, which are possible evidence of nearby prey.

# DIFFERENT HUNTING TECHNIQUES

Many sharks are masters of the ambush and take their prey by surprise in dark or cloudy waters. Some hunters, such as angelsharks, rely on camouflage to stay hidden on the seabed. The so-called mackerel sharks, including the great white, are champion swimmers and chase down prey in open water. This great white has leapt out of water after prey.

## 15 M (49 FT) AWAY

## 1 M (3.3 FT) AWAY

**Eyeing the victim**
As the shark approaches its prey, its eyes form a clear image of the target. The eyes of some kinds of shark work well even at low light intensity, helping them hunt in dark or cloudy water.

**Sensing the life**
When a shark gets close, another kind of sensing system takes over – the ampullae of Lorenzini. The ampullae are jelly-filled pores concentrated on the snout that detect the faint electrical activity of the prey's muscles and nerves, even when it tries to hide.

**Taking a bite**
Unlike most other back-boned animals, the upper jaw of a shark is not rigidly attached to the skull, so the jaws can protrude outwards. This helps the shark to take a more effective and bigger bite when it lunges forwards to attack prey.

# SHARK LIFE CYCLES

Most fish lay many eggs to improve the chances of survival of at least some of their tiny young. Sharks produce fewer offspring, and about 60 per cent of species give birth to live pups, after a prolonged pregnancy. This means the pups are born at an advanced stage of development, so have a good chance of looking after themselves. The remaining sharks produce eggs in protective, horny cases.

Some female sharks have given birth **without being fertilized**.

### Gestation

Sharks that give birth to live young do so after a pregnancy that, depending upon species, may be up to two years long. In some kinds of shark, the unborn pups are even nourished by the mother in the womb.

Sharks that give birth to live young

### Giving birth

Sharks often choose to give birth in sheltered nursery grounds, away from the danger from predators. This newborn lemon shark is still attached to its mother by its umbilical cord, the special thread that passed nutrients into the unborn pup when it was still in the womb.

### Mating
All species of shark have internal fertilization so must mate. During mating, the male bites the female to hold on and then passes sperm into her body through special grooved structures on his pelvic fins.

# GROWING UP

The habitat and even appearance of a shark can change as it grows up. Many newborn sharks spend their infancy in the shelter of shallow bays before venturing out into the deeper ocean. Young sharks of some species have striking patterns, possibly for camouflage. Zebra shark pups, for instance, lose their stripes and become spotted as they grow older. These stripes may help the pups look like sea snakes.

**Zebra shark pup**

**Adult zebra shark**

Sharks that lay egg cases

## Egg cases

Some sharks produce leathery egg cases that harden soon after release. Some cases are ridged to help them get wedged between rocks, such as the spiral casing of this bullhead shark case. Others have tassels so they snag on weed and don't get washed away.

## Growing in the egg case

Young get nourishment from their yolk sac and grow bigger inside their egg cases. The cases may take a year to hatch, but some kinds of shark retain them for longer in their body for protection, and only release them when their development is nearly complete.

# SHARKS IN OCEAN HABITATS

With a few exceptions, all sharks live in the saltwater of the ocean. Some sharks, including the most primitive kinds, prefer to stick to deep, dark waters that make up the biggest proportion of the ocean habitat by volume. Others hunt near the surface, or stay in the shallower coastal waters of the ocean's continental shelves.

## MIGRATION

Some sharks are long-distance travellers, following migratory routes that may differ between age groups or sexes. Female blue sharks cross the Atlantic Ocean, between mating grounds in the west and sites for giving birth in the east.

Mating

Pupping

**Surface ocean waters**
**0–200 m (0–656 ft)**
The clear, sunlit ocean surface supports billions of tiny animals and plants called plankton – food for filter-feeders such as whale sharks and forming the start of a food chain that ends with meat-eaters such as the great white.

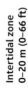

**Intertidal zone**
**0–20 m (0–66 ft)**
Where the ocean meets the land, animals must cope with the movement of tides and the crashing of waves. A few sharks, such as the epaulette shark, can survive out of water while the tide is low.

Sunlight Zone
0–200 m
(0–656 ft)

Twilight Zone
200–1,000 m
(656–3,280 ft)

**Coastal ocean waters**
**0–200 m (0–656 ft)**
Many sharks stick to the waters along the edges of continents and islands, where nutrient-rich waters can teem with prey. Females of some shark species, such as the lemon shark, give birth in shallow bays and lagoons.

**Deep ocean waters**
**1,000–4,000 m (3,280–13,120 ft)**
The deep ocean is home to bizarre animals, such as the frilled shark. Light dims into complete darkness at greater depths, through the gloom of the "twilight zone", the pitch blackness of the "midnight zone", to the "abyss" at the bottom.

**Midnight Zone**
**1,000–4,000 m**
**(3,280–13,120 ft)**

**Abyss**
**4,000–6,000 m**
**(13,120–19,680 ft)**

# SHARK FACTS AND FIGURES

Sharks are dominant predators in the world's oceans – a place they share with a huge variety of animals. They have incredible, record-breaking lives. Impressive predators, the biggest meat-eating sharks are at the top of the ocean food chain.

## SHARK HABITATS

- **Longest shark migration**: Great white shark (20,000 km/12,427 miles)
- **Longest vertical shark migration**: Pygmy shark (at least 1,500 m/4,920 ft)
- **Longest time survived out of water**: Blind shark (18 hours)
- **Deepest-living shark**: Portuguese dogfish (3,675 m/12,057 ft)
- **Shallowest-living shark**: Epaulette shark (sometimes barely submerged)
- **Smallest home range**: Blacktip reef shark (0.3 sq km/0.1 sq mile)

## SHARK LIFE CYCLES

- **Longest-lived shark**: Spiny dogfish (maximum recorded age: 75 years)
- **Slowest growth rate**: Greenland shark (1 cm/0.39 in per year)
- **Fastest growth rate**: Whale shark (as a juvenile: 46 cm/18 in per year)

**Biggest sharks shown to scale**

Great white shark (6 m/16.4 ft)

Basking shark (10 m/33 ft)

0          5 m (16.4 ft)

## THE SHARK MACHINE

- **Biggest shark to have ever lived**: *Megalodon* (20 m/66 ft long)
- **Biggest shark alive today**: Whale shark (20 m/66 ft long)
- **Second biggest shark alive today**: Basking shark (10 m/33 ft long)
- **Biggest meat-eating shark**: Great white shark (6 m/19.6 ft long)
- **Smallest shark**: Dwarf lantern shark (21 cm/8.2 in long)
- **Longest tail relative to size**: Thresher shark (half of total length)
- **Thickest skin of any animal**: Whale shark (15 cm/6 in)

## SHARKS AS HUNTERS

- **Strongest bite of any animal**: Great white shark (18,000 Newtons; a Newton is a measurement of force – the force of a bite in this case)
- **Strongest shark bite for its size**: Horn shark (338 Newtons)
- **Fastest bite**: Wobbegong (1/50 second)
- **Biggest shark teeth ever**: *Megalodon* (18 cm/7 in long)
- **Biggest shark teeth of any shark alive today**: Great white shark (7 cm/2.7 in)
- **Biggest teeth relative to size**: Large-toothed cookiecutter shark
- **Fastest swimming shark**: Short-finned mako shark (100 kph/62 mph)
- **Slowest swimming shark**: Greenland shark (1.25 kph/0.7 mph)

*Megalodon* (20 m/66ft)

Whale shark (20 m/66 ft)

15 m (49.2 ft)

20 m (66 ft)

# GLOSSARY

**Anal fin**
An unpaired fin on the underside of a fish, behind the pelvic fins and in front of the tail.

**Antenna**
A feeler-like sense organ on the head of certain kinds of invertebrate (animals without a backbone).

**Barbel**
A whisker-like, sensory organ near the mouth of certain kinds of fish, such as the sawshark.

**Bioluminescence**
The production of light by living things, caused by chemical reactions in the body. Many deep-sea animals are luminous (produce light), which helps them attract prey, distract predators, or communicate.

**Bivalve**
A shelled mollusc with a shell made up of two connected parts. Clams and mussels are bivalves.

**Buoyancy**
The ability of an aquatic (water-living) living thing to float in water.

**Camouflage**
The way the appearance of an animal, such as its colour or shape, helps it blend in with its surroundings.

**Cartilage**
A tough, rubbery material that makes up the skeleton of sharks and related fish. Most other vertebrates (back-boned animals) have a skeleton made mainly of bone with a little cartilage in places.

**Cold-blooded**
An animal whose body temperature varies with that of the surroundings. Reptiles, amphibians, fish, and invertebrates are cold-blooded.

**Continental shelf**
A region of shallow ocean water that surrounds a continent. On its outer edge, it plunges down into the deep sea.

**Crustacean**
An invertebrate with jointed legs and, usually, a hard, outer shell. Shrimps, crabs, lobsters, and krill are crustaceans.

**Denticle**
A tiny, hard, tooth-like scale on the skin of sharks and rays.

**Dorsal fin**
An unpaired upright fin on the back of a fish, whale, or dolphin.

**Echinoderm**
An invertebrate with a star-like body, hard chalky plates in its skin, and tube feet. Starfish and sea urchins are echinoderms.

**Egg case**
A tough, protective, horny casing that encloses the fertilized eggs of some sharks and rays.

**Feeding frenzy**
When a group of predators, such as sharks, gathers together to herd and attack prey.

**Filter-feeder**
An animal that feeds by straining out plankton or other small particles of food suspended in water.

**Flatfish**
A type of bony fish in which both eyes have moved to the same side of the head by the time it has become an adult. It then lives with its "blind side" facing downwards close to the seabed. Plaice and flounders are flatfish.

**Food chain**
A sequence in which energy in food passes from one living thing to another, such as when plants are eaten by herbivores, and herbivores are eaten by carnivores.

**Fossil**
The remains or traces of long-extinct animals or plants left in rocks.

**Gill**
A part of the body used by an animal to breathe in water.

Oxygen in the water moves into the blood in the gills.

**Intertidal zone**
The region of ocean shoreline that is regularly uncovered and then covered by water during the ebb and flow of the tide.

**Invertebrate**
An animal without a backbone.

**Keel**
A ridge running down each side of the body near the tail, in some kinds of fish. Keels help stabilize the fish in the water and are prominent in fast swimmers.

**Larva**
The young stage of certain kinds of animal. Usually a larva looks different from the adult form.

**Mammal**
A back-boned, warm-blooded animal, such as a human or whale. Mothers of all mammals feed their young with milk.

**Migration**
A periodic animal journey, usually to reach feeding or breeding grounds. Many ocean animals migrate across stretches of ocean, but others do vertical migration from the depths of the ocean to its surface.

**Mollusc**
An invertebrate with a soft, muscular body. Some molluscs, such as snails and clams, have a hard shell. Others, such as squid and octopuses, do not.

**Operculum**
A flap that covers the gill openings in most kinds of fish. It is not found in sharks and rays, which is why their gill slits are visible.

**Parasite**
A living thing that gets food or shelter from another, called the host, causing the other harm.

**Pectoral fin**
A pair of fins connected to the "chest" region of a fish, usually just behind the head.

**Pelvic fin**
A pair of fins connected to the underside of a fish, behind the pectoral fins and usually in the region of the belly.

**Photosynthesis**
A chemical process in plants, algae, and seaweed in which sunlight is used to make food from carbon dioxide and water.

**Plankton**
Tiny animals and plants that swim or float in water.

**Polyp**
A tiny, anemone-like, moving part of a coral. Each polyp has stinging tentacles for grabbing prey.

**Predator**
An animal that kills another animal for food.

**Prey**
An animal that is killed by a predator for food.

**Spiracle**
A small breathing hole behind the eyes of most sharks and rays. Some of the water taken into the mouth for breathing emerges through the spiracles; the rest moves out over the gills.

**Reef**
A large, rocky structure, usually found around tropical coastlines, which is formed by the growth of coral.

**Reptile**
A back-boned, cold-blooded animal with dry, scaly skin. Turtles, lizards, snakes, and crocodiles are reptiles.

**Scavenger**
An animal that gets its food by eating the leftovers of other animals.

**Tentacle**
Long, soft, moving "arms" in some kinds of animal, including octopuses and squid. They use the tentacles to catch prey.

**Venom**
A poisonous substance that harms the body when it enters through a bite or a sting.

**Vertebrate**
An animal with a backbone. Examples include fish, amphibians, reptiles, birds, and mammals.

**Warm-blooded**
An animal whose body temperature stays warm, even when the surroundings are cold. Mammals and birds are warm-blooded. A few fish, such as the great white and sailfish, are partly warm-blooded too.

# INDEX

# ACKNOWLEDGMENTS

**Dorling Kindersley would like to thank the following people for their assistance with this book:**
Charvi Arora, Esha Banerjee, Shatarupa Chaudhuri, Ateendriya Gupta, Nandini Gupta, Victoria Pyke, Rupa Rao, and Deeksha Saikia for editorial assistance; Sheila Collins, Anjana Nair, and Amit Verma for design assistance; Neeraj Bhatia for hi-res assistance; Shanker Prasad for CTS assistance; Sumedha Chopra for picture research assistance; Hazel Beynon for proofreading; and Helen Peters for the index.

**Picture Credits**

The publisher would like to thank the following for their kind permission to reproduce their photographs:

(Key: a-above; b-below/bottom; c-centre; f-far; l-left; r-right; t-top)

**2 SeaPics.com:** Andy Murch. **3 SeaPics.com:** Masa Ushioda (c). **4 SeaPics.com:** Espen Rekdal (l); Paul Whitehead (r). **5 SeaPics.com:** Doug Perrine (l); 5Mark Strickland (r). **6 Corbis:** Andy Murch / Visuals Unlimited (l). **SeaPics.com:** Masa Ushioda (r). **7 SeaPics.com:** David B. Fleetham (r); Doug Perrine (l). **10 Alamy Images:** blickwinkel (b). **Corbis:** Wil Meinderts / Buiten-beeld / Minden Pictures. **11 123RF.com:** Michael Rosskothen (cla). **12-13 Science Photo Library:** JAIME CHIRINOS (t). **14-15 FLPA:** Ian Coleman / Minden Pictures (t). **Fotolia:** rolffimages (background). **17 Photoshot:** Kelvin Aitken-V&W / NHPA. **18 SeaPics.com:** Eric Cheng. **19 SeaPics.com:** Tobias Friedrich. **20-21 FLPA:** Kelvin Aitken / Biosphoto (t). **Science Photo Library:** CHRISTIAN DARKIN (b). **24 imagequestmarine.com. 26-27 naturepl.com:** Wild Wonders of Europe / Lundgren. **28-29 Dreamstime.com:** Stbernardstudio (b). **Science Photo Library:** JAIME CHIRINOS (t). **30 Photoshot:** Gerard LACZ. **34-35 Robert Harding Picture Library:** Reinhard Dirscherl. **36-37 SeaPics.com:** Marty Snyderman. **39 SeaPics.com:** Andy Murch. **40 SeaPics.com:** Andy Murch. **41 SeaPics.com:** Amar & Isabelle Guillen. **42 SeaPics.com:** Martin Strmiska. **43 SeaPics.com:** Doug Perrine. **44 SeaPics.com:** Andy Murch. **45 Dreamstime.com:** Ethan Daniels. **46-47 SeaPics.com:** Friederike Kremer-Obrock. **48-49 Alamy Images:** Ed Robinson / Design Pics Inc (t). **50 Dreamstime.com:** Izanbar. **51 SeaPics.com:** Paul Whitehead. **52-53 SeaPics.com:** Doc White. **54-55 Photoshot:** Paulo de Oliveira (b). **SeaPics.com:** Florian Graner (t). **56-57 SeaPics.com:** Doug Perrine. **58 SeaPics.com:** Doug Perrine. **59 Corbis:** Norbert Wu. **60-61 SeaPics.com:** V&W / Kelvin Aitken (t); Andy Murch (b). **62 SeaPics.com:** Doc White. **63 SeaPics.com:** Doc White. **64-65 naturepl.com:** David Shale (b). **Science Photo Library:** Dante Fenolio (t). **64 naturepl.com:**

David Shale (cr). **65 Science Photo Library:** Dante Fenolio (ca). **66 naturepl.com:** David Shale (bl). **67 Photoshot:** Paulo de Oliveira (cl). **68-69 SeaPics.com:** Doug Perrine (t). **70 Ardea:** Steve Downer. **71 Alamy Images:** AF archive. **72-73 SeaPics.com:** Jonathan Bird. **74 Corbis:** Norbert Wu / Minden Pictures. **75 SeaPics.com:** D.R. Schrichte. **76 OceanwideImages.com:** Rudie Kuiter. **77 SeaPics.com:** Andy Murch. **78 SeaPics.com:** Jonathan Bird. **79 SeaPics.com:** Nigel Marsh. **80 Photoshot:** A.N.T. Photo Library / NHPA (cr). **SeaPics.com:** John C. Lewis. **81 SeaPics.com:** Franco Banfi. **82 Rex Shutterstock:** Gerard Lacz (cl). **82-83 FLPA:** Norbert Wu. **84-85 SeaPics.com:** Nigel Marsh (b). **86-87 SuperStock:** Minden Pictures. **88 SeaPics.com:** Andrew J. Martinez. **89 Fotolia:** Strezhnev Pavel (background). **OceanwideImages.com:** Gary Bell. **90-91 SeaPics.com:** Reinhard Dirscherl. **92-93 Corbis:** Reinhard Dirscherl // age fotostock Spain S.L. **94 SeaPics.com:** Nigel Marsh. **95 Corbis:** Andy Murch / Visuals Unlimited. **SeaPics.com:** Masa Ushioda (bc). **96-97 Alamy Images:** Evagelos Panagopoulos (b/backdrop). **SeaPics.com:** Franco Banfi (b); Mark Strickland (t). **98 Corbis:** Birgitte Wilms / Minden Pictures. **99 SeaPics.com:** Lia Barrett. **100 OceanwideImages.com:** Gary Bell. **101 Alamy Images:** HUBERT YANN (clb). **Dreamstime.com:** Francesco Pacienza / Fotoprogetto. **102-103 Alamy Images:** Jane Gould. **104-105 SeaPics.com:** C & M Fallows. **106-107 naturepl.com:** Dan Burton. **108 SeaPics.com:** Tom Haight. **109 naturepl.com:** Franco Banfi. **110 SeaPics.com:** Justin Gilligan. **111 SeaPics.com:** Stephen Kajiura (cl). **113 SeaPics.com:** Reinhard Dirscherl (tr). **114 SeaPics.com:** Andy Murch. **115 SeaPics.com:** Andy Murch. **116 SeaPics.com:** Richard Herrmann. **117 SeaPics.com:** Susan Dabritz (crb); David Shen. **118 SeaPics.com:** Masa Ushioda. **119 Getty Images:** Roger Munns - Scubazoo. **SeaPics.com:** Bonnie Pelnar (cra). **120 SeaPics.com:** David B. Fleetham. **121 Fotolia:** Strezhnev Pavel (background). **122 SeaPics.com:** Richard Herrmann. **123 SeaPics.com:** David B. Fleetham. **124-125 SeaPics.com:** Masa Ushioda. **126 naturepl.com:** Doug Perrine. **127 Getty Images:** Brian J. Skerry. **128 OceanwideImages.com:** Gary Bell. **129 SeaPics.com:** Doug Perrine. **130 SeaPics.com:** Wolfgang Poelzer. **131 SeaPics.com:** Solvin Zankl. **132-133 SeaPics.com:** Pablo Cersosimo. **134-135 naturepl.com:** Sue Daly (b). **SeaPics.com:** Doug Perrine (t). **136 naturepl.com:** Alex Mustard. **137 FLPA:** Bruno Guenard / Biosphoto. **138 SeaPics.com:** Andy Murch. **139 SeaPics.com:** Andy Murch. **140 SeaPics.com:** Rudie Kuiter. **141 SeaPics.com:** Florian Graner. **142-143 naturepl.com:** Jeff Rotman (t). **OceanwideImages.com:** Andy Murch (b). **144 Photoshot:** Jeremy Stafford-Deitsch / Oceans Image. **146-147 Alamy Images:** ArteSub (b). **OceanwideImages.com:** Gary Bell (t). **149 Alamy Images:** Masa Ushioda. **SeaPics.com:** Masa

Ushioda (br). **150-151 OceanwideImages.com:** Michael Patrick O'Neill. **151 SeaPics.com:** Andy Murch (tr). **152 SeaPics.com:** D.R. Schrichte; D. R. Schrichte (bl). **153 SeaPics.com:** Florian Graner; Shedd AQ / Brenna Hernandez (br). **154-155 Corbis:** Pablo Cersosimo / robertharding. **155 Alamy Images:** Paul Fleet (t). **156 Dreamstime.com:** Richard Lindie (bl). **Photoshot:** Steve Jones. **157 naturepl.com:** Gabriel Rojo. **SeaPics.com:** V&W / Gerard Lacz (br). **158 Alamy Images:** Cornforth Images (cr); imageBROKER / Thomas Sbampato. **159 Getty Images:** Paul Nicklen. **SeaPics.com:** Michael S. Nolan (crb). **162 SeaPics.com:** Michael Aw. **163 SeaPics.com:** Reinhard Dirscherl. **164 FLPA:** ImageBroker. **165 SeaPics.com:** Franco Banfi. **166-167 SeaPics.com:** David B. Fleetham. **168 SeaPics.com:** Reinhard Dirscherl. **169 OceanwideImages.com:** C & M Fallows. **170 SeaPics.com:** Masa Ushioda. **171 SeaPics.com:** e-Photo / Toshio Minami. **172 SeaPics.com:** Masa Ushioda. **173 SeaPics.com:** Masa Ushioda. **174 OceanwideImages.com:** Gary Bell. **175 SeaPics.com:** Jez Tryner. **176 FLPA:** Norbert Wu. **177 OceanwideImages.com:** C & M Fallows. **178-179 SeaPics.com:** Andy Murch. **180-181 SeaPics.com:** Jim Abernethy. **182 Alamy Images:** Martin Strmiska. **183 Corbis:** Reinhard Dirscherl / Look-foto. **184 SeaPics.com:** Ethan Daniels. **185 SeaPics.com:** Martin Strmiska. **186 naturepl.com:** Doug Perrine. **187 Ardea:** Colin Marshall. **188 OceanwideImages.com:** Gary Bell. **189 Dorling Kindersley:** Linda Pitkin. **190-191 SeaPics.com:** Doug Perrine. **192 Alamy Images:** blickwinkel (cla). **Dreamstime.com:** Mr1805 (cb). **Science Photo Library:** CHRISTIAN DARKIN (cl). **SeaPics.com:** Tobias Friedrich (cra). **193 Science Photo Library:** JAIME CHIRINOS (crb). **194 FLPA:** Photo Researchers (bc). **195 123RF.com:** Robert Cope (bc). **Corbis:** Norbert Wu / Science Faction (br/cookie); Jeffrey L. Rotman (bc/mouth). **Dreamstime.com:** Vladislav Gajic (tl). **SeaPics.com:** David Shen (br). **196 Alamy Images:** Masa Ushioda (cr, crb). **Dreamstime.com:** Naluphoto (cl, cl/shark). **SeaPics.com:** Doug Perrine (c, cb). **197 Corbis:** Gerald Nowak / Westend61 (cl). **Getty Images:** Barcroft (cr). **naturepl.com:** Chris & Monique Fallows (tr, clb). **SeaPics.com:** Masa Ushioda (c, cb). **198 SeaPics.com:** Jonathan Bird (cla); Doug Perrine (tc). **198-199 National Geographic Creative:** NICK CALOYIANIS (c). **199 Dreamstime.com:** Ben Mcleish (cra). **Getty Images:** Paul Kay (crb). **SeaPics.com:** Tim Rock (tc); Christian Zappel (tr). **200 SeaPics.com:** Amar & Isabelle Guille (bc); Jeff Jaskolsk (tc). **201 FLPA:** Kelvin Aitken / Biosphoto (tr). **SeaPics.com:** Eric Cheng (tl). **202 Alamy Images:** digitalunderwater.com (clb/basking); All Canada Photos (clb). **202-203 SeaPics.com:** Doug Perrine (cb)

All other images © Dorling Kindersley

For further information see:
**www.dkimages.com**